To the children
– ours and all the others

EMIL L. FACKENHEIM

# The Jewish Bible
# after the Holocaust

## A Re-reading

**Indiana University Press**
Bloomington and Indianapolis

Copyright © Emil L. Fackenheim 1990

*Library of Congress Cataloging-in-Publication Data*
Fackenheim, Emil L.
    The Jewish Bible after the Holocaust– a re-reading / Emil L. Fakenheim.
       p.   cm.
    "Based on the Sherman lectures, delivered at Manchester University in November 1987" – Foreword.
    Includes bibliographical references and index.
    ISBN 0-253-32097-8
    1. Bible. O.T. – Criticism, interpretation, etc., Jewish.
2. Bible. O.T. – Criticism, interpretation, etc. – History – 20th century. 3. Holocaust (Jewish theology). 4. Holocaust (Christian theology) I. Title.
BS1186.F36   1990
221.6 – dc20      90-5170

1 2 3 4 5  94 93 92 91 90

Manufactured in Great Britain

# CONTENTS

# FOREWORD

This book is based on the Sherman Lectures, delivered at Manchester University in November 1987. I wish to thank my hosts for their warm hospitality, and express special gratitude to Manchester University Press for waiting so patiently for a publishable manuscript.

The delay was caused mostly by the fourth chapter which, not among the lectures, had to be written *de novo*. That it was nevertheless 'first in thought' (though 'last in work')[1] the reader may find confirmed in a first version of it, published as far back as 1980.[2] A comparison of the two versions will also show readers interested in such matters how far I have come between then and now.

Through that concluding chapter Jewish–Christian dialogue becomes part of my purpose. The book's heart and soul, however, is a struggle with a two-dimensional abyss torn up in the decade between 1935 – the Nuremberg laws – and 1945 – the end of the Holocaust. One abyss is between 'non-Aryan' Jews robbed of choice and eventually doomed to a choiceless death, and 'Aryan' Christians cursed and blessed by the gift of a choice – that between acquiescing in their 'Aryan' designation and rejecting it, this latter if necessary unto death. Another abyss then rent open is between Jews and Christians, on the one side, and the respective Bible of each, on the other. If here I speak of one two-dimensional abyss, rather than of two separate ones, it is because, for the task that occupies me in these pages, the two are interrelated. And the task arises at all because, whereas the 1935–45 decade is over, the two-dimensional abyss is not: after that decade, Jewish–Christian relations cannot be what they were before; nor can the reading by either Jews or Christians of their respective Bible. I have arrived at these convictions over the years. Without them, this book would not have been written.

They give rise to the need for what may be called a post-Holocaust Biblical hermeneutic. Its task is to close the two-dimensional abyss. To perform it is probably beyond the power of the present generation, unwilling or unable as it still mostly is to even recognise an abyss. At least to narrow it, however, is a task that ought no longer to be postponed. That even to this end this volume is but a modest contribution goes without saying. So does the fact that to write a post-Holocaust Christian theology – a task for Christians – would not, here or elsewhere, enter my mind: even in this book's fourth chapter I do not lose sight of the fact that, with regard to Jewish–Christian relations, I am located on the Jewish side.

The word 'fraternal' appeared in the title of the 1980 essay, and reappears in that of the present Chapter IV. If the book had a different subtitle, however, its operative word as regards Jewish–Christian relations would have to be 'coexistence'. Evidently the Holocaust has brought Jews and Christians closer together: that it has also set them further apart is less evident, if evident at all. Yet on occasion it becomes evident enough, and it grabbed headlines in the recent Auschwitz monastery controversy. The Carmelite nuns failed to consult Jews before locating their monastery at that unique place of Jewish suffering. This bespeaks insensitivity and – theologically more importantly – an a priori view that, whatever the Holocaust may have done to the Jewish faith, it has done nothing to the Christian. This is so minimally. In a maximal interpretation, the theology of the Auschwitz monastery goes even further: it is nothing less than an attempt – one fears, not the only one – to transsubstantiate the worst Jewish catastrophe in history into a triumph of the Christian faith. This – the maximal Auschwitz monastery theology – cannot but reinforce the 1935–45 abyss. Even the minimal one – a Christian unwillingness to face up to the Holocaust as a trauma to their faith – does nothing to narrow it, when just this is the task of Jews and Christians alike.

Such a narrowing occurs, however, once Jews and Christians alike face up to the two-dimensional abyss and, in consequence, find themselves, each in relation relation to his or her Bible, – for Jews the Ta'nach, for Christians Old and New Testament – , so to speak, in the same boat. It is this possibility that encourages my attempt (in the fourth chapter) at a fraternal reading by Jews and Christians of the Book that belongs to both.

From the side of Jews, this attempt must be preceded (here in the second and third chapter) by a re-reading of their Ta'nach on their own. A re-reading: after the Holocaust, Jews cannot read, as once they did, of a God who sleeps not and slumbers not; and after the resurrection of a Jewish state that includes Jerusalem, they cannot pray for the city as though, if not there, they could not get there by an easy El Al flight. So enormous are the events of recent Jewish history – this is the central conviction informing this book's hermeneutic – that the Jewish Bible must be read by Jews today – read, listened to, struggled with, if necessary fought against – as though they had never read it before.

This must be of the 'naked text.' The term was coined, for reasons of his own, by Franz Rosenzweig before the fateful decade. After it, its meaning is more radical. Traditionally Jews build subcommentaries upon commentaries as they read their Ta'nach. This practice presupposes a continuity between past and present, between the Book then and there and ourselves here and now. A continuity between past and present is assumed also by recent general hermeneutics, and this despite its stress on the historical situatedness of both. I am close to this hermeneutics except for one crucial point: neither Paul Ricoeur nor Hans-Georg Gadamer and certainly not Martin Heidegger ever face up to the Holocaust, as an event by which historical continuity might be ruptured. What such a rupture might mean for general hermeneutics lies outside the scope of this book.[3] For a Jewish hermeneutic of the Ta'nach, it minimally means that, while commentaries and subcommentaries are still available, they, ruptured themselves, are no longer – to mix metaphors – a cushion between the reader and the 'naked' text; that, in reading their Ta'nach as never before, Jews are, as it were, themselves naked.

Toward the book's end, Germans among Christians appear prominently, even though Americans – my friends Roy Eckardt and Franklin Littell come to mind – have done so much more to expose Christians to the Holocaust. One reason is my long-held conviction that the country which produced the disease – the 'Aryan'-'non-Aryan' dichotomy – must also produce the cure – the 'Reformation' called for by Franklin Littell.[5] The other reason is personal. When in 1983 my family and I moved from Toronto to Jerusalem I never imagined that, for the first time in my life, I would teach German students in my mother tongue. *Studium in Israel* is a remarkable German enterprise that, since 1978, has sponsored annually two dozen or so Christian theological students for a year's study in Jerusalem. When in 1988, on the occasion of its decade of existence, *Studium in Israel* was awarded the Buber-Rosenzweig medal, I was asked to come to Fulda, Germany, to deliver the *laudatio*, and I accepted. It seems fitting for me to end this book with my address on that occasion, and more fitting still to add, with her permission, the response by one who, once my student, is now a *Pastorin* in Germany. I can think of no better conclusion of this volume than what I might term the anti-Bitburg note of her last sentence.

I would wish to mention numerous Jewish and Christian friends whose help has gone into this volume. They will understand why I refrain, and also why one name cannot be unmentioned, the Jerusalem director of *Studium in Israel*, my friend Pastor Michael Krupp.

# PREFACE

Is *The Merchant of Venice* a great play, a classic, inexhaustible in that it has the power to speak to every age? Not if Jean-Paul Sartre is right. In *What is Literature?* he writes that 'nobody can suppose for a moment that it is possible to write a good novel in praise of antisemitism'. Shakespeare's play may not actually praise antisemitism, but enough of it is in it – the vengeful old Jew, his daughter saved from his clutches by a triumphalist Christianity – to make it come under Sartre's judgement. One wonders whether, had it not been for the Holocaust, the so deeply-engaged French philosopher would have been so sweeping.

In *To Mend The World* (New York: Schocken, 1982, 1989) I ask but do not answer the question about *The Merchant of Venice*, literature not being my subject. Close to the core of my subject, however, is one literary work, the Jewish Bible. And if even a humanly created classic may be inexhaustible – may have the power to speak to every age – this is surely true *a fortiori* of a Book that, through the ages no mere classic, was believed to be a repository of divine Revelation. Of the Torah an ancient rabbi said: 'Turn it and turn it, for everything is in it.'

Revelation is close to the core of *To Mend the World*. At the core itself is the question of whether all Truth, Goodness, Beauty ever humanly perceived or created, ever divinely revealed, are not ruptured by the Holocaust; and if, in case this is so, a mending is possible.

*To Mend the World* first appeared in 1982. Appearing nearly a decade later, the core of the present work is the Jewish Bible, that is, the attempt at a post-Holocaust reading of it, whether by Jews alone or, fraternally, by Jews and Christians together. How to do such a reading is a question unanswerable in terms of abstract *theologoumena*, and concepts as 'the demonic' are not means of confronting but rather of evading the Holocaust. Only through an actual re-reading of Biblical texts can the question be answered – a reading of the Book as though it never been read before. Is 'everything' still in the Torah for those who 'turn it and turn it'?

Foundations for *The Jewish Bible after the Holocaust* were laid in *To Mend the World*. Foundations for the latter work, and hence indirectly also for the former, were laid yet a further decade earlier, in *God's Presence in History* (New York: Harper Torchbooks, 1972). Franz Rosenzweig's *Star of Redemption*, first published in 1921, had taught that for believing Jews – the 'eternal people,' witnesses to eternal Redemption to all humanity – nothing essential happens or can happen between Sinai and the Messianic days. Until the late 1960s I had said in my writings much the same thing. *In God's Presence in History* I could say it no more. The book affirms 'root-experiences', Salvation at the Red Sea and Commandment at Sinai, with yet a third root experience – Messianic Redemption – existing only as anticipating hope. However, jostling against these, nay, threatening them, are now 'epoch-making events', this category being second in importance in the book only to the category 'root experience' itself. That Judaism could survive the destruction of the second Temple, a catastrophe culminating in the loss of the Bar Kochba war – that it could survive in an exile with no end in sight – was not known until a response was found, in what might be called exile–Judaism. Whether Judaism can survive the vastly greater catastrophe of the Holocaust, too, cannot be known prior to a post-Holocaust Judaism that will have to pass tests, some of which we may have as yet no inkling of.

A preface that places *The Jewish Bible after the Holocaust* into the broader context of my thought seems appropriate. But the book is meant to be intelligible and defensible by itself and on its own terms.

There are more up-to-date translations of the Jewish Bible than the Jewish Publication Society version, which was first published in 1917. I have used it for the good reason that it is still seviceable, and for the better reason that it is the version most widely used among English-speaking Jews.

CHAPTER I

# The hermeneutical situation

## 1    The Christian Bible and Hegel

I must begin this book by defending my chutzpah in writing
about the Jewish Bible, when my competence is but little
greater than that of an educated Jewish layman. This is true not
only of the Bible itself but also of the rabbinic sources, some
knowledge of which is required of Jews when they open their
Bible. 'Chutzpah' (inadequately translated as 'impertinence') is
an important word in the dictionary not only of Jews but also
of Judaism. Did Abraham know what he was doing when he
called to account about Sodom and Gomorrah, not a tribal
deity, to say nothing of an idol of his own making, but none
other than the Creator of heaven and earth (Genesis.18:20 ff.)?
That he knew the enormity of his chutzpah well – shall we say
painfully well? – he showed on another occasion, this one of
lasting significance in Judaism. Not a word of protest did he
utter when this same God said unto him,

> Take now thy son, thine only son, whom thou lovest, even Isaac,
> and get thee to the land of Moriah; and offer him there for a
> burnt-offering upon one of the mountains which I will tell thee
> of. (Genesis 22:2.)

What about Abraham's chutzpah on the one occasion, his total
lack of it on the other? Jews of our time puzzled – better, most
profoundly disturbed – by this question do well to consult the
traditional Midrash.[1]

*1*

Mine is a philosopher's chutzpah, and my first line of defence is the philosophy of Hegel. I consider Hegel the greatest modern philosopher. A thinker of scrupulous integrity, he yet addressed himself to the Bible, despite the fact that his knowledge of his Bible was no greater than my knowledge of mine. (Of the rabbinic sources I can safely claim greater knowledge, for of these Hegel knew nothing.) Among Jewish thinkers I may well be a minority of one to have argued in print that, despite these limitations, Hegel had profound things to say about his Old Testament – some, possibly, not only profound but true.[2]

There is a justification to Hegel's chutzpah, as well as an explanation of the fact that he had some profound (and possibly true) things to say about his Old Testament. Both derive from the fact that his was a philosophical enquiry. He enquired into what his Bible had said, then and there, only in conjunction with considering whether (and if so how) it continued to be a repository of truth, here and now. For such an enquiry, theologians may rely on assertions, whether on grounds of sacred past authorities or deeply-made present 'commitments'.[3] Critics by profession, philosophers can respect – perhaps must take into philosophical account – assertions on both grounds; but their own discipline cannot be based on them. Even so, if Hegel may serve as an example, they may pursue their own enquiries into the Bible, and this without vainly trying to make themselves over into what could only be amateur scholars or theologians. It goes without saying, however, that some accurate idea of these disciplines may be helpful, or even necessary.

My own present enquiry into my own Bible, like Hegel's into his, is a philosophical one. And my chutzpah in engaging in it will have to be justified by the fact that I, no more than Hegel, attempt to compete with the work of Biblical scholars or theologians: by the fact that my enquiry and Hegel's are much the same kind.

But Hegel is only my first line of defence, for two reasons. The first is self-evident: Hegel was a Christian thinker, or possibly a Protestant, or post-Christian and post-Protestant one. As such (as is implied in its very title) he saw his 'Old

Testament' as superseded by his 'New'. This supersessionism is indisputably characteristic of all Christian thinkers at Hegel's time. It no longer holds true of all Christian thinkers of our own time. The exceptions, to be sure, are not very many but in my view well in advance of the rest. I have some acquaintance with the work of these, above all with their advocacy of the principle, revolutionary within Christian thought, that their Old Testament, whether or not still merely 'old' for Christians, is, and ought to remain, the ever-new Ta'nach for Jews.[4] But I have no deep familiarity with the work of those Christian theologians whom one might expect to be the very first to put this new principle into exegetical practice, namely, the practitioners of 'Old Testament Theology' or 'Hermeneutics'. (To me, the two seem in principle if not practice much the same.) Even so, I claim the right to a healthy wariness as regards that entire discipline, as well as to the chutzpah – this time Jewish as well as philosophical – of here and there testing it by examples. Looked at from outside, my examples may seem random, arbitrary or even picayune. I assure the reader, however – whatever my assurances may be worth at this stage – that for my purpose they will be none of these things.

There is a second reason why Hegel's thought is my first line of defence, and this, though equally important, is not equally obvious. In enquiring at once – nay, as it were, in the same breath – both into what his Bible said and whether and if so how it was true, Hegel tried to solve a hermeneutical problem that, given secondary variations, is still ours today. 'The Book' (whether Jewish or Christian) was written then and there. 'We' (whether Jews or Christians) are here and now. And a philosopher's hermeneutical problem is far less (if at all) the dating of the 'then and there', or the circumstances of the Book's composition, than the fact that we are in any case divorced from that 'then and there' by a history of millennia. For many (at one time most, if not all) theologians, this gap between the 'then and there' and the 'here and now' was or is of little account. It is of no account at all for Platonic philosophers and Platonising theologians – Jewish, Christian, Muslim. (To Platonists, in

3

matters of truth history is of no account: Truth is timeless, and so is the possibility of access to it; the ascent from Plato's cave, while more difficult at some times than others, is in principle always possible.) For Hegel, in contrast, access to Truth is inseparable from history, as is, indeed, Truth itself. The gap between the 'then and there' of the Book and the 'here and now' of ourselves is real.

How then did Hegel solve his hermeneutical problem? Here appears the second reason why Hegel may be my first line of defence but is only my first. *The Book was written then and there, and we are here and now: but the 'then and there', in its own right and on its own terms, is superseded because absorbed by and contained in the 'here and now'*. This, in the briefest of terms, is Hegel's stance toward his Bible at his time; but it is almost universally rejected in our time. To be sure, *mutatis mutandis* his stance is still being maintained by a few left-wing Hegelians. But of these must be said what Karl Barth said of the very first of them. For Hegel, all religions are true, though some are more true than others; and it remains for 'us' only to give to the finally true religious 'content' its finally true 'form'.[5] For Ludwig Feuerbach all religions are false, although some are less false than others; and, in giving to their falsity the finally true form, 'we' affirm an atheistic humanism that elevates Man to divinity in the same move that overcomes all past gods forever and ever. Barth accuses Feuerbach of an 'almost nauseating superficiality' concerning the Christian religion.[6] He is right in this about Christianity, despite the fact that, an ex-Christian theologian, Feuerbach knew much about the religion he had forsaken. Had Barth paid attention, he would have been more right still about Judaism, for of this Feuerbach had nothing but insulting stereotypes. This was because of ignorance but also, more importantly, because Judaism did not fit into his left-wing Hegelian scheme.

What applies to Feuerbach applies to Marx (who by his own confession relied on Feuerbach) as well as to Engels, Lenin, Trotsky, and all the rest who relied on Marx. To go further, Barth's judgement applies even to so maverick a Marxist as the twentieth-century Ernst Bloch. Bloch broke with much, not only in Marx himself, but in the whole left-wing Hegelian tradition, perhaps most dramatically so in his account of Judaism. Feuerbach, Marx and the rest had slandered the God of Judaism; Bloch goes so far as to celebrate Him. No reactionary, the 'Exodus God' is, on the contrary, the first great revolutionary. Moreover, His liberation of the Israelite slaves is not of the ancient past alone but has lived on, if precariously, through the centuries. (in heretical strains of Christianity). Bloch goes so far as to make the Messianic promise, once handed down by the Jewish God, live on in the present – for all future humanity! – as *Das Prinzip Hoffnung* – 'Hope As Principle'.

Despite all, however, this innovative thinker fails to emancipate himself from the Feuerbachian 'triviality'. In a century full of rosy expectations, Feuerbach had 'overcome' all past gods in the same act that elevated 'Man' beyond all past human limitations. On his part, Bloch 'perfects' Judeo-Christian God-dependent Messianism in the same act that transforms it into atheistic humanism. Thus he continues to elevate 'Man' at a time that, rosy no more, has seen one part of actual – not ideologised! – humanity show little response while another showed at Auschwitz a depravity hitherto believed to be beneath the humanly-possible.

'Superficiality', then, (though an endearing rather than 'nauseating' variety) characterises the thought of Bloch as much as that of Feuerbach. To compound superficiality – or is it ideological folly? – Bloch declares that, were the nineteenth century Zionist philosopher Moses Hess alive in our time, he would find his Jerusalem, not in the physical place of that name, but in the Moscow of Joseph Stalin. All this Bloch, himself a refugee from the one tyrant of this century whose crimes dwarf even those of Stalin, wrote in a place of refuge, given him not in communist Moscow but in capitalist New York.[7]

With respect to the present issue – the Bible of then and there and 'we' of the here and now – it could be argued that the only Hegelian to be taken seriously is Hegel himself.

Indeed, but for secondary variations Hegel's hermeneutical problem is still ours. However, his solution has collapsed, as will emerge, far less under the impact of subsequent philosophy than under that of subsequent events.

## 2    The Jewish Bible and Franz Rosenzweig

I must thus proceed to my second line of defence, the thought of Franz Rosenzweig. I consider Hegel the greatest modern philosopher; Rosenzweig I consider the greatest modern Jewish philosopher. Rosenzweig too was not devoid of chutzpah, and in his case, too, it was philosophical. He never acquired an extensive command of the academic Biblical scholarship of his time, spending his lamentably short life instead on matters that were more important to him. Nor did he have the time or leisure to acquire professional expertise in the rabbinic sources. Yet he had the chutzpah to claim that experts in these fields, including perhaps even his teacher, the distinguished Talmud scholar Rabbi Nehemiah Nobel, had something to learn from him. Also, as is well known, he did not hesitate to address himself to the task, together with his friend Martin Buber, of translating his Bible into German.

Rosenzweig is my second line of defence because he was a Jew, because his Jewish Bible was the Ta'nach and not the Old Testament, but also because, although broadly sharing Hegel's hermeneutical problem, he rejected its Hegelian solution. In this, to be sure, he was preceded, accompanied and followed by many others: by now their name is legion. I feel a special kinship with Rosenzweig because he preceded me in immersing himself in Hegel's thought on its own terms yet, like I, certain from the start that he would not end up a Hegelian. For Rosenzweig, then, the Ta'nach was still of the 'then and there'; 'we' were still of the 'here and now'; and the history that lay between the two was still far from Platonically-irrelevant. But now our 'here and now' neither absorbed nor superseded the Ta'nach of 'then and there'. Indeed, in one crucial respect it fell far below it. In relation to the Bible, both Jewish and Christian, Rosenzweig deliberately classified those moderns who knew their Bible, but thought of themselves as having gone beyond or – better! – 'overcome' it, together with the ancients who either had never heard its Word, or else had rejected it without really listening. Both were 'pagans' in that they rejected what to them was a 'terrible offence': the 'difference between God and man', the 'insulting' idea of Revelation – insulting because it is the 'bursting' of a 'higher [i.e., divine] content' into an 'unworthy' human 'vessel'.[8] The essential respect, then, in which for Rosenzweig the Bible was superior to ancient and modern 'pagans' alike was that it claimed to be – and for him ever more deeply became – the repository of Revelation. As a young man Rosenzweig had become disillusioned with modern culture, and hence also with the modern 'cultured despisers of religion'.[9] His disillusionment was so deep as to make him, then virtually ignorant of Judaism, come close to the portals of the church. He began to address himself to the task of a Jewish hermeneutic of the Jewish Bible of 'then and there' for our modern 'here and now' from the moment he made his monumental decision to which he gave classic expression in four words: *Ich bleibe also Jude* – 'I shall therefore remain a Jew'.[10]

The two basic questions of a hermeneutic in Rosenzweig's sense may be stated as follows: is it possible for modern man-in-general (who *qua* modern has lapsed into paganism), as well as for the modern Jew-in-particular (who *qua* modern has done likewise), to recover access to the Book of 'then and there', understood as repository of Revelation? If so, what can be done to make the possible access actual? Doubtless Rosenzweig's *Star Of Redemption* is the deepest of his several attempts to answer these questions. It must have been Rosenzweig's *Star*, more than any other work, that caused Leo Strauss to write of the late 1920s in his native Germany as follows:

It was granted by all except the most backward that the Jewish faith had not been refuted by science or by history. The storms stirred up by Darwin and to a lesser degree by Wellhausen had been weathered; one could grant to science and history everything they seemed to teach regarding the age of the world, the origin of man . . . , the Jahvist, the Elohist, the third Isaiah and so on, without abandoning one iota of the substance of the Jewish faith.[11]

The view that Strauss reports, as having been reached by his 'non-backward' contemporaries in the late twenties, I myself first reached in the same country in the late thirties; and while I yet had to understand in a depth even remotely adequate Rosenzweig's *Star*, my thinking in matters Biblical was already influenced by his shorter writings, as well as by those of his friend Martin Buber, of which more below.

In the Strauss passage, much depends on what is meant by 'the substance of the Jewish faith'. The relation of that 'substance' to the teachings of science is outside our present scope. That its relation to the teachings of history is well within it is alluded to by Strauss's mention of Wellhausen, of the Jahvist, the Elohist, the third Isaiah. I take it that in this day and age it is no longer necessary for me, anyhow a layman in these matters, to wrestle with such as Wellhausen. My friends in the field assure me that Biblical critics of our time no longer approach the 'Old Testament' in the debunking spirit so popular in the nineteenth century; and, more importantly, that they no longer bring to their supposedly unbiased scholarly activities an evolutionary scheme in which a moribund 'late' Judaism at the time of Jesus is a foregone conclusion, as is its supersession by a Christianity 'higher' in the evolutionary process. (This prejudice caused the Jewish scholar Solomon Schechter to quip that the higher criticism was the higher antisemitism.) However, if even the Wellhausen-type 'higher antisemitism' does not force one to abandon 'one iota of the substance of the Jewish faith', this is surely *a fortiori* true of the higher criticism of our time which, so my friends assure me, is antisemitic no more.

Strauss denied a conflict between Biblical criticism and the 'substance' of the Jewish faith. Yet though 'backward' already in Strauss's time, the inevitability of conflict continues to be asserted by some in our time. Before passing on, we must therefore expose the 'backwardness' of such assertions. Spinoza is generally considered the father of modern Biblical criticism. As is well known, his *Theologico-political Treatise* that contains his Biblical criticism is also, and at the same time, a wholesale (if not undisguised) assault on the (Jewish and Christian) doctrine of Revelation. Yet though the *Treatise* may refute a divinely handed-down text (with Moses on Mt Sinai acting as secretary), it never refutes Revelation: it merely rejects it. The book does not even attempt the task; and if one wants a Spinozistic refutation of Revelation, one must turn from his *Treatise* to his *Ethics*, a work culminating in the declaration that anyone who loves God truly cannot wish God to love him in turn. For Spinoza this is so for two related reasons. First, it is beneath the dignity of his God to 'descend' so as to love Man; second, it is beneath the dignity of his Man to be merely a receiving 'vessel' 'unworthy' of a 'higher [i.e., divine] content' that 'bursts' into him. For Rosenzweig, therefore, Spinoza was a modern pagan. Perhaps he was the noblest of them all. Yet if Rosenzweig could write his *Star*, it was only because Spinoza never did refute Revelation in his capacity as Biblical scholar, because he merely rejected it in his capacity as a 'pagan' philosopher.[12]

From this fact we derive a conclusion. If even Spinoza, not only the first but also the philosophically most profound of Biblical critics, could not refute Revelation – the 'bursting' of a 'higher [i.e., divine] content' into a human 'vessel unworthy of it' – by means of philological-historical criticism alone, it is safe to conclude that such a thing cannot be done. All the critics that were to follow with any such claim did not prove that the Book is a book like any other. They merely presupposed it. They deserved – and continue to deserve – the adjective that Strauss gave them when he looked back to their representatives more than half a century ago, namely, 'backward'.

They are not, however, the only ones among the backward. Perhaps it was because he had yet to understand their backwardness that, shortly after Strauss wrote what he did, J. H. Hertz, then chief rabbi of Great Britain, lapsed in behalf of Judaism into a backwardness of his own. In his *The Pentateuch and Haftorahs*, a commentary in synagogue-use for half a century (and justly cherished by worshippers well beyond the bounds of orthodoxy) Hertz wrote the following:

Judaism stands or falls with its belief in the historical actuality of the Revelation at Sinai.'[13] One considers this statement, and visualises scholars among its supporters spending their strength on refuting this or that claim of this or that Biblical critic. One can even imagine one of their number, in one person both an orthodox Jew and a Biblical scholar in a modern university, emerge with new evidence, the triumphant upshot of which is that the critics had all been wrong in their iconoclastic reconstructions of Biblical history: that the event of Sinai was exactly as the Torah reports it to have been.

One imagines this possibility – but recognises the effort of this zealous defender of Hertz's assertion to have been in vain. For proof we once more have recourse to a philosopher. In a now little-known but once powerfully-influential essay the eighteenth-century philosopher/critic/poet G. E. Lessing distinguished between 'truths of reason' (which are 'necessary') and 'truths of history' (which are at best only 'probable'). He proceeded to assert that whereas we all know about the life and deeds of Alexander the Great, no-one 'would risk anything of great, permanent worth' on this kind of truth, merely probable as it is, and then asked his climactic question, for an answer to which he looked in vain. As a Christian, he was to stake on the fact of his Christ, not merely something of 'great worth', but his eternal beatitude; yet that fact, like any other historical fact, was no more than probable. Lessing therefore went on to write: 'That, then, is the ugly, broad ditch which I cannot get across, however often and however honestly I have tried to make the leap. If anyone can help me over it, let him do it, I beg him, I adjure him.'[14] Lessing asked his question because he understood modern historiography; he would have had no need to ask it had he lived in the Middle Ages. Medieval historians accepted the past on past authority, thus encouraging a sacred historiography – Jewish, Christian, Muslim – that accepted its own past on past sacred authority. The modern-critical historian, in contrast, rejects all past authorities and *reconstructs* the past, and this on the basis of *present* evidence. However, neither his evidence nor his reconstructions can ever be final.

No matter how great his scholarly feat, then, our hypothetical Hertz-inspired Biblical scholar would fail in his religious purpose. To cite orthodox 'refutations' of modern Biblical criticism that are mere lapses into pre-modern 'backwardness' would be easy enough. But assuming our putative Hertz-defender to be a modern-critical historian, his thesis about Biblical origins would be a hypothesis, new to be sure, nay – to give it its due – the strongest yet by dint of the strength of its evidence: even so it would still be but one hypothesis among others. Because of its strength it might be dominant now. Yet *simply by being* a hypothesis it would be capable of being overthrown by a future one, stronger still. In short, Lessing has said it: 'truths of history', the part of it that is sacred included, can be no more than probable. In stating his case for Judaism in the form he did, then, Hertz meant Judaism to stand rather than fall, and to stand forever; yet precisely this 'backward' form makes his Judaism vulnerable: its hypothetical orthodox scholarly defender would make his Judaism stand today only, unable to prevent it from falling tomorrow.

The help asked for by Lessing in the eighteenth century was offered in the nineteenth in different ways by three thinkers: Hegel, Schelling and Kierkegaard. That the help offered by Hegel is no longer available we have already asserted. The help which today's Christian can still obtain from Kierkegaard (and, to a lesser extent, from Schelling), a Jew is given by the combined efforts of Rosenzweig and Buber. In a groundbreaking essay first published in 1926, Buber supports Rosenzweig's view of Revelation, and goes on as follows: 'Revelation is not a fixed, dated point between . . . [Creation and Redemption]. The Revelation at Sinai is not [the] . . . midpoint, but the perceiving of it, and such perception is possible at any time.' The ugly, broad 'ditch', then, between the Jewish Bible, then and there, and its reader, here and now, is in principle capable of being bridged because, potentially, Sinai is here and now, as well as then and there – for the reader, that is, who has abandoned modern 'paganism' and is willing, as it were, to position himself at the foot of Sinai. That this view is not altogether alien to the ancient rabbis is shown by one of their number, who asked the great question of when the Torah was given, and gave the greater answer, 'whenever a Jew receives it'. Even now truly observant Jews, who celebrate the gift of the Torah with all-night study during the Shavuot festival, act as though the ancient saying were true. Perhaps it is.

But though reckoning with paganism, the ancient rabbis did not reckon with modern critical historiography. Of the historical facticity of the event at Sinai they surely were not in doubt, nor of the Mosaic authorship of the whole Torah with, possibly, its last eight verses excepted. (These begin with 'So Moses the servant of the Lord died . . . '.) Can one surrender these facts to the uncertainties of historical reconstruction, as well as the literature that relates them to the mercy of literary critics, and still not sacrifice 'one iota' of the 'substance' of the Jewish faith, i.e., 'receive' the 'Torah' as given at 'Sinai'?

Strauss reports the Rosenzweig–Buber position correctly in asserting that this is possible. Buber begins the groundbreaking essay already cited as follows:

> *Biblia*, books, is the name of a book, of a Book composed of many books. It is really one book, for one basic theme unites all the stories and songs, saying and prophecies contained within it. The theme of the Bible is the encounter between a group of people and the Lord of the world in the course of history . . .

Much could be said (and in different contexts would have to be said) about the notions of 'encounter', of divine human encounters-in-general, and of a particular series of encounters between one 'group of people and the Lord of the world in the course of history' in particular. Sticking firmly to the present subject, we here confine ourselves to the relation between one divine-human encounter – this one supposedly crucial – and its relation, on the one hand, to its supposed historical facticity, and, on the other, to the supposed record of it contained in the 'many books' that are also 'one book'. Concerning the Revelation at Sinai Buber asks: 'What meaning are we intended to find in the words that God came down in fire, to the sound of thunder and trumpets, to a mountain which smoked like a furnace, and spoke to the people?' Buber rejects two possible answers to his own question. Of these one is that the whole account reflects a collective experience within, falsely projected on reality without: the account is 'poetry' and nothing more, and the phrase 'came down' is a metaphor without ontological truth. For the other answer rejected – it looms large in pre-modern theories, now 'backward', however – the 'came down' of the Divine is real, to be sure, but possible only as a one-time interruption of the 'natural' that is 'supernatural'. The text Buber struggles with may fairly be viewed as the central one of the entire Ta'nach. Having rejected two diametrically opposed views of it, he writes:

> [The record of the Sinaitic event] could be the verbal trace of a natural event, that is, of an event that took place in the world of the senses common to all men, and fitted into connections which the senses can perceive. But the assemblage that experienced this event experienced it as Revelation vouchsafed to them by God, and preserved it as such in the memory of generations, an enthusiastic, spontaneously formative memory. Experience undergone in this way is not self-delusion on the part of the assemblage; it is what they see, what they recognize and perceive with their reason, for natural events are the carriers of Revelation, and Revelation occurs when he who witnesses the event and sustains it experiences the Revelation it contains.[15]

Again much could (and in different contexts should) be said about this passage, charged as it is with meaning but also with ambiguity. Here no more is required than the testimony of a recent scholar:

> Whatever the experience of the people Israel on Mount Sinai was, it was so overwhelming that the texts about it seem to be groping for an adequate metaphor through which to convey the awesomeness of the event . . . What really happened on Mount Sinai? The honest historian must answer that we can say almost nothing in answer to this question . . . We know nothing about Sinai, but an immense amount about the traditions concerning Sinai.[16]

The author then turns to these traditions and – this is our point in citing him – while a scholar's objectivity prevents him from asserting that 'experience undergone in this way is not self-delusion', it equally prevents him also from denying it. Not a word in this up-to-date scholarly work (or others that could be cited) calls into question what Strauss called 'the substance of the Jewish faith', i.e., what Rosenzweig called the 'bursting' of a 'higher [i.e., divine] content' into a human 'vessel' 'unworthy' of it. A Rosenzweig alive today, with time for the task, could therefore absorb recent Biblical scholarship, yet stick with his quip about the scholarship of his time. The Book, made 'one' by reflecting the 'encounter between a group of people and the Lord of the world in the course of history,' consisted not only of many books but also, within these many, of many sources that, their authors unknown to us, were given letters in place of names by the scholars that disentangled them – 'J' for Jahvist, 'E' for Eholist, 'D' for Deuteronomist, and so on. 'R' in this scheme stood for the unknown final redactor. Of the 'R' of the Torah Rosenzweig wrote: 'We do not know the author. That it was Moses we cannot believe. Among ourselves we use the same symbol that the critics use for what they consider the final redactor, i.e., 'R'. But we complete it to say, not 'Redactor' but for *Rabbenu* – our teacher.'[17]

## 3    The Jewish Bible and Martin Buber

Rosenzweig died in 1929; Buber, having lived nearly twice as long, in 1965. A heroic task, he spent long years completing the German Ta'nach translation that the two friends had begun together. Also, unlike Rosenzweig he had spent time and effort on immersing himself in the Bible scholarship of his time. His aim, however, was not to be yet another among Biblical scholars but, so far as possible, to retrieve, for the here and now, the 'experience undergone' that had been no 'self-delusion' then and there. Works resulting from his efforts – *Moses, The Prophetic Faith, Kingship of God*, to name only the most important – are proof, to this writer at least, that what Rosenzweig thought

ought to be done can be done.

A single example must suffice. In the midst of much scholarly accounting of the nature and forms of Biblical prophecy Buber writes: 'The false prophets make their subconscious a god, whereas for the true prophets their subconscious is subdued by the God of truth, who absolutely transcends everything discoverable in the psychic domain, and Who is recognized in this very transcendence as the vanquisher.'[18] Of Buber's many works in many fields the Biblical ones bid fair, in my view, to have the most lasting influence. However, whether or not this guess will be borne out by time, their very existence is the third and last line of defence of my own chutzpah, confessed at the very start.

But, to stay with the image, these very works may well seem to reduce the space left for the fortress I wish to occupy in these pages to a vanishing point. Buber's Biblical works are not much cited by recent scholars in the field.[19] Is this because scholars are unconcerned with his purpose, or even too obtuse to understand it? Or, on the contrary, is Buber's own Biblical scholarship inadequate by the standards of our time, or even was so all along? In the first case, surely matters should be left where Buber himself left them; in the second, they should surely be carried forward by a future, better-equipped Buber. As for a philosopher, no matter how great his chutzpah, what room is left for him, when he lacks the professional expertise even to decide which of the above two possibilities is correct?

I shall cite Buber's hermeneutical principles as set forth in the 1926 essay but, for reasons that will emerge, in reverse order.

1. Once, opening the Jewish Bible in a spirit sceptical of modern 'paganism', Buber's 1926 'Man of Today' 'does not know which of its sayings and images will overwhelm and mold him, from where the spirit will ferment and enter into him, to incorporate itself anew in his body. But he holds himself open. *He does not believe anything apriori; he does not disbelieve anything apriori.*' (Italics added)

2. Rejecting a relapse into pre-modern 'backwardness',

this 'Man', to be sure, is denied the pre-modern 'certainty of faith'. (That certainty 'is not accessible to him nor can . . . be made accessible'.) But 'he is not denied the possibility of holding himself open to faith'.

3. Holding himself open – to the faith of the Book as well as to the Book itself – this 'Man' is ready, in novel ways to be sure, to resume a relation to the Jewish Bible all too hastily abandoned by modern 'pagans':

> Since this book came into being, it has confronted generation after generation. Each generation must struggle with the Bible in its turn, and come to terms with it. The generations are by no means ready to listen to what the book has to say, and to obey it; they are often vexed and defiant; nevertheless, the preoccupation with this book is part of their life, and they face it in the real world.[20]

Enunciated in 1926, how have these principles stood the test of time?

Regarding the first two principles – first listed by us but last by Buber himself – nothing has changed. 'Not believing anything a priori, not disbelieving anything a priori': who but a doctrinaire believer or disbeliever could quarrel with so open a stance to a Book that has left so profound a mark on so many centuries? 'Holding oneself open to faith': momentous though the half-century since 1926 has been, it has neither restored a pre-modern 'certainty' of faith, nor destroyed the possibility of what might be called a post-modern 'openness' to it.

But what of the principle about the Book and 'the generations'? As Buber in 1926 has it, each generation must 'struggle' with the Book on its own, a process in which there is 'vexation' and 'defiance' as well as 'listening' and 'obedience'. For all that, however, he assumes a continuity between the 'generations' – one that now is destroyed. Enormous events have occurred between then and now. This 'generation' knows. It cannot *but* know. But it has barely begun to understand. Some do understand. If these open the Jewish Bible they are more than 'vexed' and 'defiant': the Book fills them with outrage; yet, too, more than merely 'preoccupied' with it, they clutch it as if for survival. So new, so paradoxical a relation is coming into being between the Book, then and there, and the 'generation' here and now. This is because of two events, both referred to by names of places. One is Auschwitz, the other, Jerusalem.

What space, then, is left for the fortress I wish to occupy in my philosophical reading of the Jewish Bible? An abyss has been opened up between the Book, then and there, and this 'generation' here and now. Seeking to build a bridge over the abyss, I shall dwell on it; if the bridge collapses, I shall locate myself amid the heap of whatever fragments of the scaffold remain.

## 4   Post-Holocaust heirs of Buber's 'Man' of 1926

In 1926, who was Buber's 'Man of Today'? A child of modernity, he had lost the pre-modern 'certainty of faith', yet was 'open' enough to 'faith' to let the 'rays' of the Jewish Bible 'strike him' where they would: he was a certain type of central European intellectual, ready to become a believer. The designation of this very particular man as *the* Man of Today (incidentally, not only by Buber but also this 'Man' himself)[21] discloses two additional characteristics of his. First, whether Jew or Christian, his hermeneutical problem with the Jewish Bible was much the same, for he was a modern intellectual. Second, despite the catastrophe of World War I in Europe, he continued to view Europe as the centre of the world (and central Europe, as the centre's centre), for he was himself central European.

Even back in 1926, Martin Buber – after all, an early pioneer of 'dialogical' openness to another's otherness – could hardly have meant that 'preoccupation' with the Jewish Bible was 'part' of the 'life' of his 'generation' of Hindus and Buddhists. After the Second World War – a European catastrophe greater than the First – Europe is the world's centre no more. Today's world is not one but many, only some of them 'modern': there is not, then, any one 'Man' of our 'Today', but only a great, bewildering variety of men and women.

If 'preoccupied' with the 'Jewish Bible', then, today's heir, even of Buber's 1926 'Man' narrowed down to central-European-intellectual, is not one but two – a Jew and a Christian. Their heritage continues to join them together, which is why we have begun with Hegel, Rosenzweig and Buber himself, central Europeans all. This bond, however, has very nearly reduced itself to the sphere of thought, for a mere seven years later an abyss was created between them in the sphere of life that has set them apart ever since. Can the abyss be closed? Even now, half a century later, this is not certain. Yet the attempt must be made. A moral–religious necessity, an indispensable part of it are attempts at fraternal readings by Jews and Christians of at least fragments of the Book that belongs to both.

In Buber's 1926 *Man of Today and the Jewish Bible*, compared to the bonds which existed between Jews and Christians, any differences between them were small enough not even to need mentioning. Nor were those bonds a new phenomenon produced by modern enlightenment. Bonds had conjoined their remote ancestors long before the Jewish Bible ever became either a Jew's Ta'nach or a Christian's Old Testament, i.e., in Biblical times themselves. (There was shared interest, even loyalty, between Mordecai and Ahasverus; friendship between Naomi and Ruth; blood-relation between Moses, Zippora and Jethro.) When the Book became a Jew's Ta'nach and a Christian's Old Testament, this bond, to be sure, was strained; yet it remained unbroken, even in times of Christian Jew hatred since, after all, at its deepest this hatred was motivated by the Book claimed by both.

The bond was broken when a new Germany identified Christians as 'Aryans', and Jews (including converts to Christianity) as 'non-Aryans'. First defined and legislated in Germany in 1935, the 'Aryan'/'non-Aryan' separation soon became an abyss, involving directly all of Nazi-occupied Europe, and indirectly the whole world. The 'Aryan'/'non-Aryan' abyss was a *novum* in history.

The *novum* was a caesura in the history of Judaism, Christianity, and the relation between them. 'Non-Aryan' Jews were singled out for defamation, persecution and eventual murder: the *novum* for them was to be subjected to a process that *limited* and in the end *destroyed all choice*. For 'Aryan' Christians, in contrast, the *novum* was the *gift of a choice: they could accept or reject their 'Aryan' designation*. In acquiescing and accepting, they willy-nilly endorsed the 'Aryan'/'non-Aryan' abyss, nay, willy-nilly widened it. A closure would have come to pass had Christian multitudes – led by pastors, priests, bishops, theologians, all recognising a *kairos* that was theirs – brought down the 'Aryan'–Christian/'non-Aryan'–Jew distinction – brought down the Third Reich! – with the Onward-Christian-Soldiers-Battle-Cry 'Now we are Jews!' This, however, did not happen: neither the churchmen and theologians nor the multitudes recognised the hour of their visitation. And since the many acquiesced in their 'Aryan' designation, the abyss created by their acquiescence could not be closed by the few who rejected it. Identifying with 'non-Aryan' Jews, helping them in word and deed, *in extremis* trying to save Jewish lives at the risk of their own, they could not close the abyss but only, as it were, leap across it, revealing in the act what it was: *if Christians succeeded in saving a Jew's life they were Christian heroes, while the saved Jew was only a survivor; and if they failed they were Christian martyrs, while the murdered Jew only a victim.*

Jews of today are heirs of the 'generation' for which choice was destroyed; Christians, of the generation to which a new choice had been given – both of the many who, acquiescing in their 'Aryan' designation, abandoned the 'non-Aryan' Jews to their fate, *and* of the few who identified with them unto death. After what has occurred, the existence of Jews cannot be what once it was. Neither can that of Christians. Neither can the relation of the two to each other. Neither can their reading of the Jewish Bible, whether by each separately or, fraternally, by the two together.

## 5    Christian Old Testament hermeneutics after 1945

Among Christians who made the choice of the few was Dietrich Bonhoeffer. He had left Nazi Germany for America in 1939, but

returned prior to a war he saw coming. If he was to share in the
post-Nazi rebuilding of Christianity in Germany, he wrote to
the late, great Reinhold Niebuhr, he was under an obligation to
share the devastation that was sure to precede it. Bonhoeffer
did not survive for his self-imposed task. Following his return,
he followed its logic by joining a plot on Hitler's life. In 1943 he
was caught, imprisoned and, in the dying days of the Third
Reich, condemned to death and executed. Bonhoeffer – he did
not think of himself in these terms – was a Christian martyr. But
he was also a great theologian.[22]

In 1979 I enquired what, had he lived, might have been
Bonhoeffer's post-Holocaust Christian theology. (Since Bonhoeffer never knew the worst, my question was purely specula-
tive.) When Bonhoeffer was alive, Eberhard Bethge had been
his friend. In 1967 he emerged as the author of his definitive
biography. His massive *Dietrich Bonhoeffer* is the product of
years of painstaking research. Yet in response to my query he
felt impelled to question all things all over again. At length, at
the Third International Bonhoeffer Forum, he presented *Dietrich Bonhoeffer und die Juden*, a paper so electrifying as to cause
the decision to make this the sole subject of the Forum that was
to follow. On that occasion Bethge's new contribution bore the
title *Nichts Scheint Mehr in Ordnung* – ('Nothing, It Seems, Is In
Order Any More'). The title speaks volumes.

In his first essay Bethge claims no more than that Bonhoeffer is 'among those who made a post-Holocaust Christian
theology possible': since his late friend was ignorant of the
worst, nothing more was to be expected. His second essay bears
the title it does because, even forty years after, Bethge sees few
signs of a post-Holocaust Christian theology worthy of the
name. The times seem not ripe even yet; nor will they ever be
ripe unless there is first an *Erschuetterung* ('shock') in the
collective Christian soul, caused not by theologising about the
Holocaust but by the event itself.

Of post-World-War-II Christian theology Bethge writes
the following: 'Bonhoeffer would have been incapable of imagining how nearly seamlessly theology and church carried on after

1945 where they had left off in 1932.' In referring to 'theology and church', beneath Bethge's notice are theologians and churchmen who, having become Nazi or near-Nazi in or soon after 1933, abruptly became anti-Nazi in 1945, whether with or without superficial confessions of guilt. Beneath notice too – though for different reasons – are lesser figures. The judgement he attributes to Bonhoeffer applies only to the steadfast, and among these only to the great. It is the 'seamless' continuation of their theology by these that, if Bethge is right, Dietrich Bonhoeffer would have been incapable of imagining.[23]

Paul Tillich had opposed Nazism before 1933, both politically and theologically. In 1933 he left Germany for America, where he spent the rest of his life. In the Great War the warring Christian nations had all invoked God in their behalf. This, so Tillich had subsequently judged, had been idolatry. Love-of-nation is a good, but only God is ultimate. Generalising, Tillich had defined idolatry, modern style, as making ultimate what is at most only penultimate. Tillich continued to be open to new events and new challenges, through World War II and beyond. Yet when in the early 1960s he came to Toronto, he was a disappointment. He repeated his modern-style definition of idolatry as though nothing had occurred since World War I to call it into question. *But what is 'penultimate' about the Holocaust?* Bethge was right. Tillich's concept of idolatry had been important enough to him to make him oppose the Third Reich and leave it. Yet in precisely this concept, his theology remained 'seamless'.

Tillich left Nazi Germany. Rudolf Bultmann stayed on. As early as in May 1933 he warned his students against the 'idolatry of the nation', mentioning Jews as among the victims. Uncompromised at the beginning, he remained so to the end. His anti-Nazi record, like Tillich's, is impeccable.

Yet in 1949 Bultmann published 'Promise and Fulfilment', an essay which declares the 'desire of Judaism' to be at once both 'the people of God' and a 'national community' to be a 'self-contradictory phenomenon', an 'illusion' and a 'paradox'; the 'true Israel' to be 'no longer an empirical historical entity'; and, since the New Testament 'fulfilment' was quite other than that 'promised' by Old Testament 'prophecy', what had been a Jew's Ta'nach through the ages to have been, all along, a 'miscarriage'. Four years had passed since the revelation of the death camps. A Jewish state was in its birthpangs even as 'Promise and Fulfilment' was being written and published. Yet for Bultmann's theology, so far as Jews and Judaism were concerned, nothing had changed. Like Tillich's concept of idolatry, so Bultmann's 'Old Testament Hermeneutics' remained 'seamless'.[24]

Like Bultmann, Karl Barth expressed himself in public in 1949. He began his (subsequently published) radio talk, 'The Jewish Problem and the Christian Answer' with a brief nod of approval towards 'the Jewish bid for independence made in Palestine'. Then he made what for a Christian theologian was a momentous assertion. Christians have always viewed 70 CE as the Jewish catastrophe *par excellence*: destruction and exile were punishment for rejecting the Christ. In 1949 Barth was unorthodox enough to state that the year 70 had been dwarfed by the years 1933-45. For Barth, then, something new was happening in Jewish existence in 1949, and something monstrously new had happened between 1933 and 1945. Thus his 'Jewish Question' of 1949.

His 'Christian Answer', however, left no doubt that nothing new either was happening or needed to happen in Christian theology. Barth had mentioned that Jews were making a 'bid for independence in Palestine'. Yet, a 'shadow' of a nation ever since rejecting their Saviour, a shadow they remained and would remain, for they had 'no culture of their own', and the Hebrew renewed in Palestine was 'but a kind of Esperanto'. Thus wrote Barth, the theologian. How would Barth the man have fared had he tried to read a modern Hebrew poem, or merely to buy a bus ticket in Tel Aviv? So 'crass' an 'empirical' test never seems to have entered his theological mind. Concerning the Jewish event of 1949, then, Barth's theology remained 'seamless'.

It remained so also concerning the event that had ended four years earlier, his recognition of its momentousness notwithstanding. God had been faithful to His chosen people. He had remained faithful even when the people itself had become faithless by rejecting its Saviour. To be sure, for people minding their facts a new, twelve-year-long *kairos* had just occurred, in which, on the one hand, Jews had been robbed of all choice, including that between faithlessness and faith, while, on the other hand, God's faithfulness had not been in evidence. But these facts did nothing to change Barth's Christian perspective: in this, evidently Jews remained faithless so long as but a single surviving Jew failed to accept the Christ, while on His part God was faithful so long as but a single Jew survived the gas chambers. Quite consistently, therefore, Barth's 1949 Christian 'answer' to his Jewish 'question' culminates with the statement that, if Jews themselves are 'not so ready to accept the fact that they can live only by God's grace', it is because they fail to acknowledge 'the one Jew', i.e., the Christ.[25]

The worst Bonhoeffer never knew. Neither did Barth in 1942, the year in which he published his major theological statement about Jews and Judaism. To ask of this text the question I asked Bethge about Bonhoeffer is fruitful for several reasons. First, Barth was the theological soul of the Protestant anti-Nazi resistance in Germany, or what there was of it. Second, his is widely considered the greatest, most comprehensive systematic theology in Christianity since Thomas Aquinas. Third, his 1942 'Israel' in his 'Israel and the Church' is anathema not to Nazified Christian theologies only. Barth's Old Testament is alive. So are his Jews of 1942, for God's promises do not come to naught. (Israel may reject her own chosenness, yet God's chosen people she remains.) Indeed, if divine Grace did not keep the 'old Israel' alive, the 'new' could not live on its own. Less than this is enough to make Barth a 'Jew-lover' in many Christian theologies even now. Less than this was enough to earn a theologian expulsion from Nazi Germany, and worse if unprotected by a Swiss passport.

Such, in *Church Dogmatics* II 2, is Barth's promising start. In retrospect it makes what follows all the more distressing. 'Israel cuts itself off from God's community and goes into the ghetto' – written at a time when, cut off since 1933 from 'Aryan' Christians, 'non-Aryan' Jews were being herded into ghettos by 'Aryans', Christian as well as pagan. 'The Church as the coming form of the community of God has taken up into itself and therefore saved from annihilation Israel as its passing form' – written at a time when the actual Israel – the flesh-and-blood people, not a theological construct – *was being* annihilated, even as the Church, while claiming to be the coming community of God, was losing credibility as never before. 'Israel is the people of the Jews which resists its election' – written when the actual 'people of the Jews' had the best reason ever to reject its election, and yet nameless victims, martyrs despite all, accepted it with their dying breath.[26]

Barth wrote this and worse in or before 1942. What can be said of it half a century later? In charity that, even as his church was being visited by a new *kairos*, its greatest theologian knew it not; in truth, that no road leads from this 'Israel and the Church' to a post-Holocaust Christian theology. Indeed – to go to the core – , no road leads to *any* post-Holocaust theology, Jewish or Christian, from a theology armed with apriori immunity to each and every event that might threaten it. On his part, Barth openly claimed such immunity for his *Church Dogmatics* when he wrote: 'It is self-evident that everything we have said can be said and understood only in the light of the Church as the New Testament form of the community of God.'[27] In crucial respects, then, Barth's theology, like Tillich's and Bultmann's, remained 'seamless'. Throughout his career Barth theologised *about* Jews. Only toward the end of his life did he try to engage in dialogue *with* Jews.[28] By then, however, so far as his vast theological edifice was concerned, it was too late.

It had not been too late for Dietrich Bonhoeffer. 'They have burned all the houses of God.' (Psalm.74:8). This verse he underlined in his Bible, with the date November 9, 1938 scribbled in the margin. The synagogues were burning all over Germany during the so-called *Kristallnacht* and, to Bonhoeffer, synagogues were houses of God. Escalating its treatment of Jews, the regime began mass deportations two years later. Then

Bonhoeffer wrote a passage, the like of which 'is not found [in his writings] before': 'The expulsion of the Jews from the West involves the expulsion also of Christ, for Jesus Christ was a Jew.'[29]

This was cited by Bethge in his *Bonhoeffer und die Juden* at the Third International Bonhoeffer Forum. 'An Answer' to Bethge's paper was give by William Jay Peck at the Fourth. His 'answer' is *betroffen* ('struck', 'confounded', 'amazed', 'perplexed',) by a 'syllogism' that emerges from Bethge's disclosure: 'If the expulsion of the Jews from the West means the expulsion of Christ, what of the annihilation of the Jews (which began a few months later)? Here the syllogism breaks off, and we hear Bonhoeffer speak of suffering with God's suffering in a world without God, just before he sealed his own testimony with his own death.'[30]

## 6    The Jew of today and the Jewish Bible

Once Prague was a thriving Diaspora community. There, back in 1911, speaking 'as a Jew to Jews' and himself on his road to a renewal of Judaism, Martin Buber had given his first three *Reden Ueber das Judentum*. Other such *Reden* had followed soon after, inspiring a Jewish renewal in a whole generation.

Forty years later, in 1951, speaking once more 'as a Jew to Jews', Buber gave his last three *Reden*, this time, however, not in Prague. That once-thriving Diaspora community had been murdered, as had nearly all the others in Europe. Buber gave his last *Reden Ueber das Judentum* in the 'centre' of what was left of the Diaspora, New York.

In 1911 Buber had been on the road. By 1923, having reached his essential goal, he gave it classic expression: 'What is this that is eternal: the primal phenomenon, present in the here and now, that we speak of as Revelation? Just this, that a person does not emerge from the moment of the highest encounter the same as he was when he entered it.'[31]

The 'highest encounter' is with the Divine. As a 'higher [i.e., divine] content' bursts into an 'unworthy [i.e., human] vessel', a person emerges radically transformed, for the wonder is that the encounter is possible at all. How can Revelation be 'eternal' when yet each human 'here and now' differs from every other? Because – so Buber wrote in the joy, perhaps ecstasy, of discovery – the God who speaks into *this* here and now speaks into *every* here and now: because He – He alone – is the 'eternal Thou'.

Events compelled Buber to write differently thirty years later: 'Eclipse of the light of heaven, eclipse of God – such indeed is the character of the historic hour through which the world is passing.'[32] No longer – this in addressing philosophers in 1952 – is it possible to think of God speaking into *every* here and now. Addressing Jews in New York one year earlier in *At the Turning*, (his last three *Reden Ueber das Judentum*), he lets the key issue emerge in the last, climactic *Rede, The Dialogue between Heaven and Earth* – in its own climax in a question just prior to the end. 'Dare we recommend to the survivors of Auschwitz, to the Job of the gas chambers, 'Thank ye the Lord, for He is good, for His mercy endureth forever'? (Psalm 118:1,29.) Buber is right in turning to Job, and also in invoking a 'naked' text of the Book. But he never answers his own question, nay, even fails to state it adequately. The 1940s, 1950s and even early sixties, we have seen, were too soon for Christian thinkers of the stature of Tillich, Bultmann, Barth: they were too soon also for a Jewish thinker of the stature of Buber. Were Buber's question of 1951 adequate, it would die with the last survivors. But the question has not died, cannot die. For a new Jewish 'generation', and Jewish generations to come ever after, are not 'the Job of the gas chambers': they are Job's children.[33]

# Two types of murmurers: re-reading the Jewish Bible after Auschwitz

## 1    A history that almost was not

The history of the Jewish people, still far from ended, is long. It extends without interruption over nearly four millennia. Yet it almost came to an abrupt and violent end before beginning in earnest, with the Egyptian army in hot pursuit behind and, in front, impassable waters. But then, as the Torah has it, a 'strong east wind' blew 'all that night,' parted the waters so as to let the pursued pass between, but stopped blowing so that 'the waters returned,' drowning the pursuers (Exodus 14: 21-2, 28). Thus the history of this people could begin, and take its course.

Exactly what occurred, the scholars tell us, we do not know. That something momentous did occur is indubitable. Traditional Jews, of course, do not doubt it. But neither do Biblical scholars. They view the 'Song at the Sea' that follows the account of the event as among the oldest pieces of the whole Bible: they take it seriously. Still more seriously is it taken by observant Jews, who recite it twice daily in their prayers.

This reciting may be routine. Whenever it is not, however, the event that allowed Jewish history to begin serves as a paradigm of all subsequent Jewish history or, more precisely, of all those events that, time and again, averted catastrophe. But note this: so far as the Song is concerned, that 'strong east wind' that blew at just the right time, and stopped blowing at just the right time, was not a case of lucky coincidence: it was a saving act of the God of Israel.

Who is like unto Thee, O Lord, among the mighty? Who is like unto Thee, glorious in holiness, Fearful in praises, doing wonders? (Exodus 15:11.)

Twice daily Jews at prayer recall the paradigmatic event: to them it is a 'miracle'. 'The concept of miracle,' writes Martin Buber, 'permissible from the historical approach, can be defined at its starting point as an abiding astonishment . . . Any causal explanation [does not end but] only deepens' it. For Jews at prayer the astonishment continues to abide. For if the God who had saved at the beginning were not Saviour still, their own twice-daily recital of the Song would not exist today, for they, the reciting Jews, would themselves not exist.[1]

## 2 Incident at Marah

The 'Song at the Sea' is a classic. By any literary standard it deserves a separate chapter. Yet 'R' places at its end an incident that seems trivial by comparison:

And Moses led Israel onward from the Red Sea, and they went out into the wilderness of Shur. And they went three days in the wilderness and found no water. And when they came to Marah, they could not drink of the waters of Marah, for they were bitter . . . And the people murmured against Moses, saying, 'what shall we drink'? (Exodus 15:22-4.)

The narrator goes on how Moses cried unto the Lord, how the waters were made sweet, why and how the Lord had tried them, at this place called 'Marah', that is, 'bitter'. It takes the narrator just fifty-four words to relate the whole incident.

Rosenzweig, along with Buber, 'completes . . . ["R"] to say not "Redactor" but *Rabbenu*'. Following their lead, we ask: does *Rabbenu* commit a literary blunder when he places the report of the Marah incident with the great and mighty Song at the Sea? Is the Marah incident trivial?

## 3   From Marah to Massah and Meribah, and back

We turn to the next of the numerous murmurings of the Israelites in the desert, for lack of drink, food or both:

> There was no water for the people to drink. Wherefore the people strove with Moses and said, 'Give us water that we may drink', and Moses said unto them, 'Why strive ye with me? Wherefore do you try the Lord?' And the people thirsted there for water . . . and murmured against Moses, and said, 'wherefore hast thou brought us out of Egypt, to kill us and our children and our cattle with thirst.' (Exodus 17:1-3.)

Both at Marah before, and now at Massah and Meribah, Jewish history nearly comes to an end once more, though these two times not abruptly and violently, but slowly, unviolently, if no less painfully. Both these times, too, salvation occurs. The two incidents, then, have much in common, and some scholars view the two texts as 'doublettes', i.e., as different sources referring to the same incident. But *Rabbenu* – for traditional Jews '*Moshe Rabbenu*'[2] – has always disclosed an important difference. At Marah God tries Israel; at Massah and Meribah it is Israel that does the trying, not only of Moses but also, beyond him, of God Himself. So great is this difference for observant Jews that, whereas Marah is remembered just once every year in the regular Shabbat Torah reading, the Massah–Meribah incident is remembered each and every week. The Shabbat eve liturgy begins with Psalm 95. This contains the following passage:

> Harden not your heart as at Meribah, as in the day of Massah in the wilderness, when your fathers tried Me. They tested Me, although they had seen My work. (Psalm 95:8-9.)

The difference outlined, then, has always loomed large for Jews at prayer. For Jews today, however, two other differences between the two incidents bid fair to loom larger still. At Marah the people murmur; at Massah and Meribah, not forgetting even their cattle, they murmur on behalf of their children. And whereas the narrator simply relates what occurs at Marah, in relating the Massah–Meribah incident he goes further: he takes sides with Moses and God, and condemns the murmurers.

More 'pious' than the narrator, shall we condemn the murmurers at Marah also? 'Only three days since the great and mighty Salvation at the Sea,' so one seems to hear preachers lament through the ages, 'yet their faith crumbles at the very first trial!' The preachers may be Christians whose Old Testament is *Heilsgeschichte*[3] and nothing else. That they may also be Jews is shown by the following homily: 'It says, "They could not drink the water because it was bitter."(Exodus 15:23.) Bitterness was not the actual condition of the water. Rather, the Israelites felt bitter and, therefore, whatever they tasted was bitter to them.'[4]

The narrator and *Rabbenu* notwithstanding, then, are the murmurers blameworthy at Marah also – indeed, more so than at Massah–Meribah, since water was there all along and, except for their impious bitterness of soul, perfectly drinkable?

This is the Hasidic view just cited. Jews of this 'generation' are within their rights if they reject it, and do so with vehemence. They hark back from Massah–Meribah to Marah. They wonder why *Rabbenu* places this incident with the great and mighty Song at the Sea. It is not trivial after all, they discover, for there is meaning in the fact that the narrator refrains from castigating the murmurers. This is discovered by Jews of this 'generation', for as they return from the Massah–Meribah- to the Marah text, they bring to this latter a new perspective: the children.

## 4    From Marah once more on to Massah and Meribah

The waters of life are sometimes bitter, and no art or religion can make them sweet. But religion can help us drink bitter waters without being embittered ourselves. The highest point personal religion can reach is when it is possible for us to add the second clause to the first in the great text, 'O Father, if it be possible, let this cup pass from me; nevertheless, not as I will, but as Thou wilt.'[5]

The words of the 'text' cited in this passage, 'great' to be sure, are those of Jesus, and *The Interpreter's Bible* in which it is cited is addressed primarily to Christians. That it can be meaningful also for Jews has sufficient warrant in the author of the passage just cited. J. Coert Rylaarsdam was respected for his Old Testament scholarship. He also loved the Jewish Bible, its people and their descendants, right up to his own Chicago contemporaries.

Simon-pure scholars may dismiss *The Interpreter's Bible*, shot through as its hermeneutic is with homilies. A philosopher cannot follow their example, for his quest, like that of the homilist, is for a bridge between the Book, then and there, and its reader, here and now. Like the scholar, he will dismiss bad homilies; but he cannot be hostile to the homiletical enterprise.[6]

Nor, if Jewish, can he dismiss without further ado the homily just cited, and this not only despite the – in the context gratuitous – reference to Jesus, but also despite his ample and weary familiarity with Christian symbolising of Old Testament texts. (In the above homily the waters of Marah become 'the waters of life'.) For first, as already shown, Jews too may be given to symbolising; and, second and more importantly, in this particular case, at first sight, none but a symbolising hermeneutic seems possible. For if suburban dwellers in Skokie or Westchester, whether Jewish or Christian, turn on their taps and find their literal water literally bitter, they will complain, not to God but to the city water department.

This holds for Jews and Christians whose religious situation is still what it was in 1926, for the reader then addressed by Buber as the 'Man of Today'. But what if momentous events have occurred between then and now? What of Jews and Christians for whom these events have altered the religious situation radically, so that a 'seamlessly' continuous reading of the Jewish Bible has become impossible? For any such breakthrough, we have seen, it was too soon in the 1940s and 1950s, even for the great among Christian theologians. 1951 was too soon also for the Jewish thinker Martin Buber. As for the volume of *The Interpreter's Bible* that contains Rylaarsdam's Exodus commentary, it was published in 1952.

Is it still too soon now?

Today Christians read the Marah text: will they not think of African children without food and drink, receiving neither, dying of hunger and thirst? And if cite Jesus they must, will it not be for his love of the forsaken, much rather than his 'personal religion'?

Today Jews read the Marah text: will they not think of the the Warsaw Ghetto? Its waters were polluted and stayed polluted: they were not made drinkable, to say nothing of having been – except for bitterness of soul – drinkable all along.

The hermeneutic advised by Martin Buber in 1926 asks each 'generation' to struggle with the Jewish Bible, even at the cost of emerging with a mixture of 'vexation' and 'defiance', on the one hand, though 'readiness to listen and obey,' on the other. Must not Jews of this generation, on the one hand, 'listen' when the narrator of the Marah text assigns no blame to the murmurers? And must they not, on the other, be 'vexed' by the divine trial? The great and mighty Salvation had indeed occurred at the Sea: what difference does this make three days later to the mothers, when their children are dying of thirst?

Moving from Marah to Massah–Meribah once more, this generation's 'vexation' must surely escalate and turn into outright 'defiance'. The narrator takes sides with Moses, with God, and castigates the murmurers while, for their part, these murmurers invoke the children. As this is read by Jews of this generation, they perceive just how radically their religious situation has changed: they have no choice but to take sides with the mothers of the children, against the narrator, against Moses and, if necessary, against God Himself.

## 5    Korach

To side with Biblical murmurers is one thing. To side with them *just because* they are murmurers would be quite another. To side against the narrator, against Moses, if necessary against God Himself remains within a hermeneutic that lets 'each generation' be 'vexed' and 'defiant' in its struggle with the Jewish Bible, so long as 'occupation' with it remains 'part' of its 'life'. But to side against the narrator, against Moses, against God *simply and solely because* they *are* who they are would bring any such 'occupation' to an end. In any such doctrinaire stance, fashionable to be sure, what would remain of an 'openness' to the 'many books' rendered 'one Book' by 'encounters' between a 'group of people and the Lord of the world in the course of history'? What of a stance that neither 'believes a priori' nor 'disbelieves a priori'? The Book would become a relic from the dead past.

> It is of a past of this kind now, if sides are taken with Korach: Now Korach, the son of Izhar, the son of Kohath, the son of Levi, with Dathan and Abiram, the sons of Eliab, and On, the son of Peleth, sons of Reuben, took men; and they rose up in face of Moses, with certain of the children of Israel, two hundred and fifty men; they were princes of the congregation, the elect men of the assembly, men of renown; and they assembled themselves together against Moses and against Aaron, and said unto them: 'Ye take too much upon you, seeing that all the congregation are holy, every one of them, and the Lord is among them; wherefore then lift ye yourselves up above the assembly of the Lord?' (Numbers 16:1-3.)

A Jewish philosopher, I read this text, and what comes to mind are left-wing Hegelians who transform the Biblical liberation *of* a people *by* God into human *self*-liberation *from* God. To mind, too, come Nietzscheans for whom the death of God paves the way for man's self-elevation to over-humanity. Why these? Because the issue in Korach's murmuring is holiness: not the holiness attributable to God but the holiness accessible to humanity.

Korach considers himself holy. So do Dathan, Abiram and all the rest. Do they consider the entire congregation holy? So they say, and the reason given is that the Lord dwels among them.

Does Moses consider himself holy? One prophet, Amos, is a herdsman whom the Lord takes from following the flock (Amos 7:14–15). As another, Isaiah, sees the Lord sitting on 'a throne high and lifted up', he becomes a man of unclean lips in his own eyes (Isaiah 6:1, 5). Yet a third, Jeremiah, when receiving his first divine Word, protests that he on his part has no words, being but a child (Jeremiah 1:6). What of Moses, 'the chief of the prophets'?

> The man Moses was very meek, above all the men that were upon the face of the earth.' (Numbers 12:3.)

Yet now he is charged by Korach with having 'lifted himself up above the assembly of the Lord'. And the reason given is that all are holy, for the Lord dwells among them.

Can humans attain to holiness? Whatever phraseology is used, the answer is affirmative both for left-wing Hegelians since Feuerbach, and for Nietzscheans since Nietzsche himself. They and their disciples – direct and indirect, authentic and unauthentic or even perverse – call on humans to raise themselves above all past limits of humanity. In the first case, all past gods can and must be 'overcome'; in the second, it is possible and necessary to recognise their death. Future humanity, then, achieves holiness – or what throughout history was called by that name – if and when it takes the place once occupied by the Divine. Korach and his followers, on their part, consider themselves holy even now, for 'the Lord dwells among them'.

This is the ground of their murmuring. Yet the prophets all testify that, while God may dwell amid the people, He is neither a human possession-in-general nor a Jewish 'monopoly'-in-particular.[7] Being human, the people are but 'vessels' 'unworthy' of a 'higher [i.e., divine] content' that might 'burst' into them; as for holiness, it is accessible to them only if they recognise themselves for who they are. Meant here by holiness, of course, is a human form of it, not the holiness attributable only to God.

The definition of Revelation just alluded to was given by Franz Rosenzweig in an essay written less than half a year after his *Ich bleibe also Jude*. The year was 1914; the time, just prior to the outbreak of the Great War. The point of 'Atheistic theology' – a title shocking no more, but shocking at the time, and meant to shock – is that Revelation is an 'offence' to modern as well as ancient pagans, and so much so to the former that this unprecedented thing has come to pass that theology, evading if not denying Revelation outright, has itself become atheistic. Rosenzweig ends his essay as follows: '[Jewish or Christian] theology may be as *wissenschaftlich* as it can be and wants to be: the thought of Revelation it can no longer evade.'

One ponders Rosenzweig's timing and marvels at his perspicacity. An ominous course of events was even then set in train that would climax in the triumph of ill-begotten offsprings of left-wing Hegelians, on the one hand, of Nietzsche, on the other, all having one thing in common: the arrogating unto themselves of a holiness attributable only to God.[8]

From the prophets we have turned to Rosenzweig. From Rosenzweig we turn back to the 'chief of the prophets'. Moses has heard Korach's charge. He falls on his face. Then he rises to speak, saying these words:

> Know ye that the Lord hath sent me to do all these works, and that I have not done them of my own mind. (Numbers 16:28.)

Can Jews of this 'generation' do other than take sides against Korach? Do they have any choice but to side with the narrator, with Moses and, if possible, with God Himself?

## 6    Hovering

Jews of this generation think of the victimised children – and side with the mothers among the Biblical murmurers, against the narrator, against Moses and, if necessary, against God Himself. They think of the children's 'pagan' victimisers – and side against Korach among the Biblical murmurers, with the narrator, with Moses and, if possible, with God Himself. Like Jews of other 'generations' as they 'struggle' with the Book, they are ready to both 'listen and obey', and be 'vexed' and 'defiant'. But so unprecedented is their religious situation that a hovering between two types of Biblical murmurers has come into being that is itself without precedent.

## 7    **The spies**

The narrator is markedly more severe on murmurings subsequent to the Sinai event than on those prior to it. This is important, and the scholars have duly noticed it. No less important, however, is that his severity is special when at stake in the murmuring are not survival needs only – lack of food or water, threats posed by enemies – but also destiny. This is the case with the Land.

Moses dispatches twelve to explore it. The people murmur when they hear the report of ten of them, and their punishment is savage: they will not live to enter the Land, the 'evil report' which they have believed.

Why does Moses have the Land explored, when Abram (not called 'Abraham' yet) to whom it is first promised is prepared to get out of his 'country', his 'kindred', his 'father's house', all this knowing no more of the Land than that God would 'show it' to him? (Genesis 12:1-5.) This question must been asked through 'the generations', by readers known and unknown. To Jews of this generation the thought occurs that whereas Abram and Sarai (not called Sarah yet) are still childless, Moses is the steward of families. Do mothers not have a right – nay, the duty – to know into what kind of country they will take their children? A country divinely promised, to be sure, but a country unknown?

The twelve have all seen the same land, but they have not seen it the same way. That it flows with milk and honey all agree, but whereas two, Joshua and Caleb, urge 'going up at once to possess it', as seen by the ten it is 'a land that eats its inhabitants'. Inhabited by giants, the spies were like grasshoppers in their eyes; they were like grasshoppers in their own eyes as well. To be sure, Joshua and Caleb rejoin that with God's help these giants will be 'bread' for His people. Yet the people listen to the ten, murmur and indeed go beyond murmuring: they plan to choose a captain who will take them back to Egypt. (Numbers 13, 14:1-4.)

The narrator sides against the ten and the murmurers, and with Joshua and Caleb; and so, as the Ta'nach has it, do Moses and God himself. Moreover, this stance was to be shared by generations of readers who, exiled from the Land, never ceased to pray for a return to it. This they did despite their knowledge of the price paid by their ancestors for entering and dwelling in it. For, in the eyes of the exiled descendants, what were Canaanites and Jebusites, Amalekites and Philistines? Were even Babylonians and Romans 'giants', the ones, having brought about a past Jewish exile, the others, one still present? What did all these matter, compared to 'going up to the Land' – the one piously remembered by the exiled generations, the other prayed for with ceaseless fervour?

> Even if the Land were in heaven and He were to say, 'Make ladders and go up there', we should listen to Him because we would be successful in all He bids us to do. (Rashi ad Numbers 13:30.)

Thus writes Rashi (1040-1105), the most widely-read and beloved of traditional commentators.

Past generations have prayed for a new 'going up to the Land'. This generation has gone and done it. It has paid a price, continues to pay it, and dare not forget those who paid it with their lives. Already hovering between two types of murmurers in its struggle with the Book, this generation therefore finds itself torn still further when it re-hears the report of the spies. 'Going up' once more, it has found the Land, to be sure, flowing with milk and honey. (So the twelve all have it.) But it has also found it *both* (as the two have it) an 'exceedingly good Land' *and* (as the ten have it) one that 'eats its inhabitants'. Jews today, then, cannot take sides – simply, piously – with Joshua and Caleb; indeed, in some respects they must side even *against* them. In the view of these two, the enemies, giants as seen by the ten, will be 'bread', i.e., devoured by His people with God's help. Having 'gone up' once again, however, this generation would not want to make some – Palestinian Arabs – into 'bread' even if it could. As for others – Syrians, Iraqis, Libyans, Algerians, Iranians and the rest of an immense multitude – they are so gigantic as to render absurd any thought of making them into bread: the ten have spoken of giants, and giants these multitudes are. Nor do they hesitate to view those who have 'gone up' as grasshoppers: they have gone up, they say among themselves if not to Western media or politicians, but with patience and 'steadfastness' will be made to go down again.[9]

This Jewish generation, then, is torn between the two reports and hovers between them. In one respect, however, there can be no hovering but only a steadfast siding with Joshua and Caleb, with the narrator and, as the Ta'nach has it, with God Himself: the Jewish generation that has gone up to the Land once more may not be like grasshoppers in its own eyes.

This generation hovers. But, then – so Jews today discover, or rediscover – so does the generation of the desert itself. They wish to return to Egyptian slavery. This is how they begin, grasshoppers in their own eyes. But how do they end? They repudiate their plan. They will not live as slaves in Egypt but die in the desert, free men and women. This they choose on account of the children. The children will not be slaves in Egypt. Neither will they die in the desert. They will live and, free men and women, enter the Land.

## 8    The Golden Calf and the hovering of Moses

> And when the people saw that Moses delayed to come down from the mount, they gathered themselves together unto Aaron, and said unto him: 'Up, make us a god who shall go before us; for as for this Moses, the man that brought us up out of the land of Egypt, we know not what is become of him.' (Exodus 32:1.)

'What has become of him': why do the people voice this fear of theirs only when Moses 'delays' to 'come down' from Mount Sinai? Why not, when he 'goes up', at once?

> And Moses went up into the mount, and the cloud covered it for six days; and the seventh day He called unto Moses out of the midst of the cloud. And the appearance of the glory of the Lord was like devouring fire on the top of the mount in the eyes of the children of Israel. And Moses entered into the midst of the cloud and went up to the mount . . . (Exodus 24:15-18.)

The people see a cloud cover the mountain; they see what appears in their eyes like devouring fire; they see Moses enter into the midst of the cloud and go up: why do they not bring their fears to Aaron at once? This is the wonder.

In contrast, no wonder is caused by the fact that, when the delay is great and they do speak up, they ask not just for a new 'man' like 'this Moses' to 'go before them', but a god.

> Before them went the Lord . . . by day in a pillar of cloud to lead them the way, and by night in a pillar of fire to give them light. (Exodus 13:21.)

This happened while Moses was among them: now, with Moses vanished into that cloud, has not his God vanished with him? They are leaderless, lost in the desert. They would be less than human if they were not afraid, and inhuman if they did not fear for their children. While it lasted, then, their patient faith has been admirable; and now that it has come to an end, the request they make is understandable. So at least it is, or ought to be, in human perspective.

Yet, as the Torah has it, in divine perspective their faith and patience are insufficient. As for the request that follows the breakdown of both, it is the one sin reported in the entire Ta'nach so heinous as to merit extermination – the death not only of responsible adults but also their children. There is no extermination unless it includes the children. On Moses' part, his 'delay' to come down is considerable:

> And Moses was in the mountain forty days and forty nights. (Exodus 24:18.)

We know little of Sinai, but much of traditions about Sinai.[10] About the forty days and nights Moses spent on the mountain, even the traditions are scanty. That no more occurred than the gift of the commandments listed in Exodus 25-31:17 is out of the question, a fact recognised by the rabbis when they make the 'more' into the Revelation of the 'oral' as well as the 'written' Torah. This too, however, falls short of adequacy, even given the rabbinic view that the oral Torah, to be studied by humans forever, is inexhaustible: what happens between Moses and the divine Glory in the stark immediacy of those days and nights is incommunicable. The reticence of the tradition is thus not accidental: one cannot communicate the incommunicable. Yet by any religious standard even remotely adequate, those days and nights are the apex of Moses' entire life, and hence – he is the 'chief of the prophets'! – of the Ta'nach as a whole.

Forty days and nights Moses, a mere human, is alone with a 'Glory' that is like devouring fire in the eyes of other humans: how is it that he is not devoured? He is a prophet, and a prophet communicates. He is the chief of the prophets. In the presence of a Glory that is incommunicable, he rises even above prophecy: does he rise to over-humanity?

'Man is not a goal but a bridge, between animal and Overman': thus teaches the deepest of modern 'pagans'. But for Nietzsche's Zarathustra God is dead, whereas the 'Glory' that descends on Mount Sinai, fire-like, is alive – and with this Moses dwells for forty days and forty nights. 'Man is . . . but a bridge between the ape and the Overman', Zarathustra proceeds to insist; and, with God dead, for the bridge, so to speak, to cross itself – so as to get to the other side – is the sole alternative to decadence for the many and despair for the few. 'What theology must think,' writes Rosenzweig, 'is the God who builds the bridge between Himself and the people and all humanity.' In his solitariness with the divine Glory, those long days and nights of it, does Moses rise to over-humanity? He does not, is the only possible reply, for it is God who builds a bridge, and this to Moses in his humanity; and as, subsequently, he descends from the mountain, he himself becomes a bridge between God and 'the people and all humanity'.

> When He made an end of speaking with Moses upon Mount Sinai, He gave unto him the two tables of the testimony, tables of stone, written with the finger of God. (Exodus 31:18.)

Moses himself is a bridge: in his descent he brings with him two tables, the writing on which is communicable – to 'the people and all humanity'. But note this well: the writing is by the finger of God.

'Unworthy [i.e., human] vessel of a higher [i.e., divine] content': never does Moses experience this fact so deeply – uniquely! – as during those days and nights on the mountain. Never is he so close to Divinity, and hence so remote from his people in their humanity. Hence as, descending, he finds them all-too-human, the clash between him and them is radical. In human perspective, their behaviour is understandable. The perspective in which the descending Moses sees it can only be divine. 'Break the tables, break them,' Nietzsche's Zarathustra keeps urging his 'friends'. Perceiving, it seems, the spectre of dire things to come if the 'everyone and no one' addressed does not listen – *or does* listen! – , his urgency, near-hysterical, increases as he comes close to the end of his speeches: the tables, man-made, must be broken by Man on his road to over-humanity. In contrast, the tables Moses brings from the mountain, are not man-made and – this in further contrast – are brought to 'the people and all humanity' *in* their humanity. Yet Moses too wants them broken, nay, does this bold thing never thought of by Zarathustra: he breaks them himself. Subsequently, to be sure, the people are given a new set of the tables. But note this well also: this new set is not written by the finger of God.[11]

As he breaks the tables Moses is at one with the wrath of God. In His own wrath, however, God goes further. He will do nothing less than exterminate the people, man, woman and child; yet, lest the history begun with the Wonder at the Sea come to a fruitless end, He will continue it with Moses – with him alone and his seed.

The days and nights on the mountain are Moses' great moment above history: the greatest of his many great moments *in* history is surely his response to this divine threat of extermination. In breaking the tables written with the finger of God, he has sided with God against the unworthy people; now that this people is to be exterminated, he sides with them, unworthy though they are, against God Himself. What will the Egyptians say of a God who, in breach of His own promises, brought His people forth from their land, only to slay them in the mountains? (Exodus 32:12-13.) Moses asks this question when first learning of the divine threat. When he is asked to save the divine reputation – the history begun in earnest with the Wonder at the Sea will continue, through Moses and his seed – he, as it were, blackmails God.

> And Moses returned unto the Lord, and said: 'O, this people have sinned a great sin, and have made them a god of gold. Yet now, if Thou wilt forgive their sin – ; and if not, blot me, I pray Thee, out of Thy book which Thou hast written.' (Exodus 32:32.)

One cannot imagine Moses wishing to die unless it is with his whole people, man, woman and child. Nor can one, for a lesser cause, imagine him, 'meek above all men who were upon the face of the earth', blackmail God.

Jews of this 'generation' hover between two types of Biblical murmurers, siding with some but against others. When reaching the supreme crisis-moment in the entire Ta'nach – at stake is Jewish survival itself – , they discover that Moses himself hovers. They also discover that, in response to Moses, God Himself hovers as well, between a Wrath that would exterminate and a Mercy that forgives.

On a subsequent occasion – the incident of the spies already considered – Moses pleads with God once more. That time, however, he need not be torn between siding with God against the people, and with the people against God: he is able to cite God against God. Among divine qualities, he pleads, are Grace as well as Justice, not only a wrath that would destroy but also a love that forgives. God responds as follows:

> I have forgiven according to your word. (Numbers 14:20.)

These words are cited on Kol Nidre. Kol Nidre initiates Yom Kippur, the apex in Jewish religious life on which Jews – this on behalf of 'all humanity' – anticipate Eternity.[12] If extermination did not befall the desert generation for the extreme sin – paradigmatic for sin-in-extremity ever since – , it will not befall their descendants ever after. Jews on Yom Kippur can anticipate Eternity on behalf of 'all peoples', for they are an eternal people.

9    **On reading the Ta'nach in retrospect**

> . . . and if not, blot me, I pray Thee, out of Thy book which Thou
> has written. (Exodus 32:32.)

'Thy book', we have assumed, is the book of life. This is assumed
also, among other traditional commentators, by Nahmanides
(1195?–1270). But Rashi takes the 'book' to be the Torah: his
Moses wants his name 'blotted out' of the Book in which it
appears so prominently and which, as tradition has it, – except
possibly for the last eight verses – was written by him as dictated
by God. Why? Rashi goes on: 'in order that people should not
say about me that I was not worthy enough to pray effectively
for them.' What people? Those about to be exterminated, just
prior to it happening? One asks this question of Rashi. Of
Nahmanides one does not ask it, for this is how he interprets the
divine threat: 'I will erase from my book [of life] whosoever
sinned, but not you, for you have not sinned.' Moses has not
sinned: have the children? The God of Nahmanides, then, does
not threaten extermination, after all, while Rashi's Moses (who
recognises the threat) responds to it weakly: he dissociates his
name from its execution, but goes no further. Neither 'pious'
commentator, then, dares hold together the 'naked' text's God
who does threaten extermination and its Moses who views this
threat – it does include the children! – divinely issued but
humanly intolerable and unacceptable. In the incident of the
spies we have seen Moses go along with a wrathful God who will
let the sinful generation die in the desert; but when, in the case
of the golden calf, He threatens extermination – the death of the
sinless children – , the Moses of the 'naked text', meek, faithful
and indispensable servant though he has been, goes so far as to
blackmail God. We ourselves have added the traditional
*k'b'yachol* ('as it were') in using so 'blasphemous' a word. As for
Rashi, Nahmanides and the bulk of the traditional commentators, no word suggesting the idea, however euphemistically
disguised, would cross their lips. Why are they more 'pious' than
the Biblical narrator, its Moses, the Biblical God Himself? Why
is it necessary, how is it possible?

One expects such piety from Christian commentators, handicapped as they have been through the ages by leaping from saint to saint in reading their Old Testament, so as to reach their Christ. In contrast to a Christian's Old Testament, however, the Ta'nach of Jews is the record of their own flesh-and-blood people, men, women and children. Yet we have found samples of Jewish piety exceeding that of the text throughout the present discourse. Why, then – to hark back to our very first example – castigate the murmurers at Marah when the Biblical narrator does not?

Many answers are possible. Only one is good: *through the 'generations' Jewish readers have read their Ta'nach – nay, their whole past history – in retrospect.* Even so, to be sure, this past has looked precarious enough: the Hanuka hymn includes the ominous phrase 'I almost perished.' Yet that hymn is one of celebration: divine salvation has never failed, not from slavery in Egypt, not from exile in Babylon, not from Haman's plot, not from a Syrian oppression that meant to wipe out both Jews and Judaism. Often enough salvation came at the last moment, but come it always did. The Hanuka hymn is loved by the children.

The *Dayyenu* too is loved by the children. This hymn is part of the Passover Seder liturgy, and as close to a *Heilsgeschichte* as Jewish liturgy ever comes. Going far beyond the Hanuka hymn, it recounts the acts of divine Grace from the Exodus to the gift of the Land and the Temple in Jerusalem, adding each time that, had God's Grace ended with the act just cited, – *Dayyenu*, 'it would have been enough for us'. The Dayyenu contains the following stanza:

> Had He split the sea for us, bringing us safely through it without even getting our feet wet, and not caused the pursuing oppressors to be engulfed in its deepening waters, it would be enough for us.

But would it have been? Of course not, for the 'oppressors' would have gone on with their 'pursuit', wiped out a Jew's ancestors, and left no distant ones now to sing either the Hanuka hymn or the *Dayyenu* itself. The religious truth even of the Hanuka hymn, and certainly of the *Dayyenu*, is thus retrospective: until the Messianic rebuilding of the Temple, divine salvation will always come in time; no matter how often it may seem otherwise, 'He that keepeth Israel sleepeth not and slumbers not'. (Psalm 121:4.)[13]


## 10  Rupture

'Sleepeth not and slumbers not': the Psalmist finds it possible to say these words of a God who keeps Israel, even if often at the last moment. Chaim Kaplan found it necessary to say them of an enemy bent on her extermination, and succeeding beyond the limits of previous imagination, the Biblical included.

Whether Kaplan knew the worst is unknown for, rather than sent to Treblinka, he, resident, observer and diarist of the Warsaw Ghetto, may already have been murdered in the Ghetto itself. That what he did know was enough to warrant the above-cited words emerges from the diary itself, as painstakingly factual an account as has survived, of the actions of the sleepless enemy, of the suffering of his victims, of the quest evident on every page of a God whose sleeplessness would match that of the enemy. 'The naïve among the Jews and Poles ask: "Can the world sit silent? Will the evil and the corrupt always have the upper hand? Will the axe fall upon the entire world? O Leader of the city, where are you?" But He Who sits in Heaven laughs.' Thus writes Kaplan as early as 24 October 1940, a man, unlike others, naïve no more. He is careful to add that it is the night of Simhat Torah, the day of rejoicing of the Torah, 'the same Torah,' he continues in an entry the day after, 'for which we are murdered all day, for which we have become like lambs to be slaughtered.' The Simhat Torah day entry contains also the following: 'A large number of zealous Hasidim on Mila Street . . . sang holiday songs in chorus out in public . . . Joy and revelry in poverty-stricken Mila Street!' Some went on singing even when warned that they were endangering their lives.

These are early entries. One of the last is dated 23 July 1942. The 'relocations' were well under way. Kaplan was not deceived by this euphemism. 'We remember the words of the elegist: 'On this night my sons will weep.' In these two days [of mass deportations] the emptiness of the ghetto has been filled with cries and wails. If they found no way to the God of Israel, it is a sign He doesn't exist.' 'A sign,' writes Kaplan. Note well that even in this extremity he does not write 'decisive proof'.

What concerned Kaplan more than his own survival was that of his diary. 'Some of my friends and acquaintances who know the secret of my diary urge me, in their despair, to stop writing. "Why? For what purpose? Will you live to see it published? Will these words of yours reach the ears of future generations? How?"' Kaplan reviews their reasons for rightly considering his diary's survival improbable, yet goes on:

> I refuse to listen to them. I feel that continuing this diary to the very end of my physical and spiritual strength is a historical mission which must not be abandoned. My mind is still clear, my need to record unstilled, though it is now five days since any real food has passed my lips. Therefore I will not silence my diary.

Kaplan's last words are: 'If my life ends – what will become of my diary?' Against all odds the diary survived. It was published. Even so, Kaplan's last hope has been fulfilled thus far only in part. The book is available. But theologians, philosophers, historians and ordinary folk have yet to read and understand it as read and understood it must be.

Adam Czerniakow's *Warsaw Ghetto Diary* is of a different order. Kaplan, an educator and writer, could not act but only observe. Czerniakow could not *but* act; for reasons he may have come to regret, he had allowed himself to be thrust into the position of president of the *Judenrat*. Some may have taken such posts in the hope of saving themselves. Czerniakow took it in the hope of saving others, consenting to do bad things in the hope of averting worse: his hope, however, proved vain. There is no precedent in literature for tragic heroes such as Czerniakow, for there is no precedent for them in life.

An entry in his diary dated 22 July 1942 – as it happens, almost the same date as Kaplan's just cited – reads in part as follows:

Sturmbannfuehrer Hoefle and associates came at 10 o'clock . . . Children were moved from the playground opposite the Community building. We were told that all the Jews irrespective of sex and age, with certain exceptions, will be deported to the East. By 4 p.m. today a contingent of 6,000 people must be provided. And this (at a minimum) will be the daily quota.

Czerniakow had carried poison on his person through the entire period of his post as *Judenrat* president. The day after this order he took it. Editor Raul Hilberg writes:

> The survival of the children was the ultimate test of his efforts in the Ghetto. It has been reported that after Czerniakow made his last entry in his diary on July 23, 1942, he left a note to the effect that the SS wanted him to kill the children with his own hands.

Czerniakow loved the children. This, if little else, he shared with Kaplan, the author of Hebrew books for children, still in print, it is said, in the United States. When Kaplan heard of Czerniakow's death he wrote: 'He did not have a good life, but he had a beautiful death . . . There are those who earn immortality in a single hour . . . Adam Czerniakow earned his immortality in a single instant.' Once Moses offered his life in behalf of the children and succeeded. Adam Czerniakow did not merely offer but gave his life for the children. However, unlike Moses he failed. The enemy was more sleepless and slumberless than the God of Israel.

## 11   The situation

In 1951 Martin Buber wrote of the 'Job of the gas chambers'. Nearly outdated then, he is wholly outdated now. This Jewish 'generation', and those to follow, are of Job's children. As such they can no longer read the Ta'nach – read their whole history – in the age-old, time-honoured, venerable, pious retrospect. This they might if the disaster that struck Job – struck the Job of the gaschambers – had spared the children. However, the children – not those that are the Jews of today – are dead. Hence, to be sure, with eyes to Jerusalem, Salvation may be said to have come once more. But this time, for the first time, it came too late.

# Sacred scripture or epic of a nation?: re-reading the Jewish Bible in Jerusalem

## 1 An inscription on a wall

> I will take you from among the nations, and gather you out of all the countries, and will bring you into your own land. (Ezekiel 36:24).

This verse from the Jewish Bible is inscribed on the main wall in the main hall of *Beit ha-Nassi*, the 'House of the President' of the State of Israel in Jerusalem. Attending meetings or listening to lectures, I have sat staring at that passage many times, pondering its meaning – not for the Hereafter or the End of Days, nor in the mind of either God or the prophet Ezekiel, but just this: its meaning as inscribed at this time on that wall.

This verse belongs to every place and no place, to every time and no time, Mahatma Gandhi in effect declared, well before the State was ever proclaimed or that verse inscribed. He did so by publicly declaring that Zion – he called it 'the Palestine of the Biblical conception' – was not a 'geographical tract' but was 'in the heart' and nowhere else.

The timing of Gandhi's declaration was singularly unfortunate. Perhaps it was this fact, or it combined with the reverence he felt for the Indian leader, that led Martin Buber to respond to his public declaration himself publicly, and this with uncharacteristic bluntness.

> A land about which a sacred book speaks to the sons of the land is never merely in their hearts; a land can never become a mere symbol. It is in their hearts because it is the prophetic image of

*49*

a promise to mankind: but it would be a vain metaphor if Mount Zion did not actually exist. This land is called 'holy'; but this is not the holiness of an idea: it is the holiness of a piece of earth.

Buber wrote this and much more in his letter to Gandhi who, on his part, had himself written much more. But a reply to Buber he never wrote.[1]

Gandhi was not a Christian. Even so, his view expresses to perfection a Christianity liberal in the extreme: if Jerusalem can exist in the green fields of England and the prairies of America, why not anywhere-in-general – and nowhere-in-particular?

At its opposite extreme, a good many Christians have no difficulty with the 'piece of earth', the 'existing' Mount Zion, and the return to both of the flesh-and-blood Jewish people. Indeed, quite a few, visitors at *Beit ha-Nassi*, must have nodded happy approval on having that passage translated. To them, however, it is the harbinger of the returning Christ, and it need hardly be said that this is not its meaning, either for the President of the Jewish State, or for the people he represents.

The search for the meaning of that text at this time on that wall is not advanced significantly if we turn from Christian to Jewish extremists. For a Jewish view liberal in the extreme, Jews ought to exist everywhere and nowhere, and in every time and no time, that is, make themselves over into mankind-in-general or – in case they rush hither and thither in search of 'mankind' but fail to find it – at least into a vanguard of its future.[2] Its radical opposite, an extreme Jewish orthodoxy, complicates a complex matter still further in that it falls itself into extremes. At an anti-Zionist orthodox extreme – anti-Zionist even when located in Jerusalem, indeed, there above all – there is no trouble with the Ezekiel passage: it is affirmed with fervour. However, its inscription at this time in that place is considered blasphemous, as is, indeed, the Jewish state itself. To be sure, the exiles will be returned to the Land: such is the divine promise. This will be, however, by the God-appointed Messiah not, taking matters into their hands, by such as David Ben Gurion or Golda Meir. Meanwhile – even after the Holocaust – it is religiously necessary for exiled Jews to stay exiled.

If residing in the Jewish state, they must therefore boycott it, pray for its demise, and do so even at as outlandish a place as Tehran, and as outlandish a time as the funeral of the Ayatollah Khomeini.[3] Obviously, no enlightenment comes from this quarter as to the significance of that Ezekiel passage, as inscribed at this time on that wall.

One fares only slightly better with the other extreme of current Jewish orthodoxy, for which the re-establishment of the state is no less then the 'beginning of the growth of the [Messianic] redemption'. In itself this formula is neither extreme nor exclusively orthodox: in the cautious formulation just cited (part of a prayer for the state authorised by the Israeli chief rabbinate), it is recited in many non-orthodox synagogues the world over. In its incautious interpretation, however, it does not refer to the state's existence only, with any 'growth' of 'redemption' precarious, arrested by lapses, and altogether ambiguous: some ultra-orthodox interpreters possess a veritable map of a divine plan. What was the meaning of the 1947-8 Israeli War of Independence? To restore a Jewish state after nearly two thousand years of statelessness! Of the 1967 Six-Day War? To return the whole Land! Of the Yom Kippur War? To punish the people for their sins! One wonders what the far-from- thoughtless author of the book referred to would say about the divine purpose of the 1982-3 Lebanon War. (His book was published before then.) And – this in charity – one refrains from imagining what on his map of divine plans might be the meanings of the Holocaust.[4] Even a Zionist Jewish view orthodox in the extreme, then, does not help much as one ponders the significance of that passage on that wall.

It would not help too much more even if, more cautious, it let go of maps of divine plans. Israel is a Jewish state, but it is also a democratic one. Its president represents not only religious Jews, to say nothing of ultra-orthodox ones, but all of the state's citizens, the majority of whom consider themselves secularists, and a minority – not now, or ever, to be ignored – are not Jews at all. Israel would cease to be herself if she ceased to be a Jewish state; but this would be true also if she ceased to be a democracy.

This latter assertion depends not on Western-type commitments alone, such as to freedom of speech, to duties owed to minorities, to the right of citizens to a share in their government: in short, on the modern Western belief in democracy as the best government in a world that can have no perfect government. The majority of Israel's Jewish citizens are refugees from countries not known for their democracy. (Of these most, from Arab countries; a good many, from the Soviet Union.) Their conversion to democracy ought to arouse admiration. The speed of it, however, would make it vulnerable if democracy were a Western import only; and it is under threats, even now, from extremists among the ultra-orthodox, who now and then drop hints that one day, running a properly Jewish state at last, they will get rid of democracy as an alien import.

But democracy is no alien import into either Zionism or the Jewish state: it is of the essence of both. At its noblest and best, modern secularism consists of human self-reliance, of doing away with reliance on others, of taking one's destiny into one's own hands. At its noblest and best, too, this self-reliance is shown not by 'movements' led by Robespierre or Napoleon, Lenin or Mussolini, all acting on behalf of 'the masses', but rather by movements without such leaders and, no mere 'masses' but rather, whether rich or poor, learned or simple, workers or entrepreneurs, composed of individuals acting on their own. Theodor Herzl was no Robespierre or Napoleon, Lenin or Mussolini, representing Zionist 'masses'. He did not have the power and, had he had it, would not have been ruthless enough to use it. It was individuals who packed up and left oppressive Russia and Poland, Iraq and Syria, and – most recently – Iran and Ethiopia, this in order to reach, not the golden promise of America or Canada but the hardships of the Land which – so the Jewish Bible asserts – was once promised to Abraham and his seed. It was individuals, too, who left a promise fulfilled in the 'new lands' of America or Canada, so as to help open, in the old Land, a new chapter in Jewish history. By any standard even half- honest, half-decent, then, the modern Zionist movement is not only among the most noble expressions of modern secularism but also among its most democratic. What makes it revolutionary within Judaism, however, is the fact – it ought to provoke deep if doubtless disturbing theological thought – that the 'others,' from dependence on whom this revolution emancipated itself include the ultimate Other – the God of Israel.

Perhaps the best thought yet provoked is that of Abraham Isaak Kook (1865-1935), chief rabbi of the Ashkenazi Jewish community of Palestine from 1919 to his death. Orthodox though of course he was, he perceived a pious spark even in the most atheist Jews who 'went up' to the Land to replant and rebuild it. Israel would cease to be herself if she ceased to be a democratic state; Kook perceived that she would cease to be herself also if she were no longer a Jewish state. The impulse that created the state – that continues to animate it – differs from other such impulses creating and animating other modern secular states. True, without that self-reliance Jews exiled in Russia and Poland, Iraq and Syria, Iran and Ethiopia would be exiled still, whether waiting for the old God or the New Man to liberate them. (Alternatively, having given up on both and assimilated, they might have vanished.) Yet without an ancient religious impulse – dormant and obscure for centuries but now come powerfully alive – there would be neither Zionism nor a Jewish state rebuilt in the old-new Land. Secular Zionists – 'Zionists' no longer – might have built a state in Uganda, one doomed soon to cease to be Jewish if not cease to be; not a state, however, bound to remain Jewish, in the Land to which – so the Ezekiel passage at that wall in the House of the President declares – God Himself would return His people Israel.[5]

## 2  Does God remember?

The passage on that wall refers to the most recent turn in Jewish history. Let us hark back to its most ancient beginning and, like those responsible for that inscription, have recourse to the Ta'nach:

The Jewish Bible after the Holocaust

> And it came to pass in the course of these many days that the king
> of Egypt died; and the children of Israel sighed by reason of the
> bondage, and they cried, and their cry came up unto God by
> reason of the bondage. And God heard their groaning, and God
> remenbered His covenant with Abraham, with Isaac and with
> Jacob . . . (Exodus 2:23-4.)

This passage describes a 'turning point' in the history of the
Jewish people. Going along with modern critics, one might
describe it as marking its very beginning, with Genesis being
myth or pre-history – that of a 'family' expanding into a tribe,
and ending with four centuries of slavery in Egypt.

'God remembered': had He forgotten? [6] Heaven forfend,
pious commentators may protest, for is He not the Guardian of
Israel who sleepeth and slumbereth not? (Psalm 121:4.) Is He
not, as the most beloved of psalms has it, the One Who is with
us even though we walk through the valley of the shadow of
death? (Ps.23.) Some psalms, however, strike a quite different
note:

> Thou hast given us like sheep to be eaten;
> And hast scattered us among the nations.
> Thou sellest Thy people for small gain,
> And hast not set their price high.
> Thou makest us a taunt to our neighbours,
> A scorn and a derision to them that are round about us.
> All the day is my confusion before me,
> And the shame of my face hath covered me . . .
> All this has come upon us;
> Yet have we not forgotten Thee,
> Neither have we been false to Thy covenant . . .
> Nay, but for Thy sake are we killed all the day.
> We are accounted as sheep for the slaughter.
> Awake, why sleepest thou, O Lord?
> . . . Wherefore hidest Thou Thy face,
> And forgettest our affliction and oppression?
> (Psalm 44:12-14, 16, 18, 23-5.)

Elsewhere in the Writ holy to Jews and Christians, it is God who
remembers, who sleeps not and slumbers not. Here, in the same
Writ, it is Israel that both is awake and remembers, whereas He

who is God of both Jews and Christians is asleep, having forgotten.

Accustomed to reading their Old Testament both in the light of the New and selectively, worshippers among Christians may skip such psalms. Their Old Testament scholarly theologians may not skip; yet, safe both in their seminaries and a Christ who has 'overcome the world' (John 16:33), they may feel free to dispose of such psalms as 'bumptuous'[7] expressions of an insufficient faith. Jews, their scholars included, lack this particular freedom. A flesh-and-blood people inclusive of children, they do not live in the safety either of theological seminaries or of a-world-overcome. Nor did King David, traditionally viewed as the author of most psalms, even of Psalms as a whole. This tradition, though unaccepted by scholars, has a certain poetic truth. Like Psalms itself, David, mighty and exalted king though he is, is *with* his people, their fears and their hopes, their moments of anguish and those of joy. In legend he will lead his people in song when all fear and anguish will be of the past, when the time will have arrived for the Messianic feast.

The psalm just cited is near-desperate. Yet despair does not enter – fragment, destroy – the Jewish faith. God *does* remember: this commitment has its most authoritative liturgical expression in the *Zichronot*, the 'Remembrance-Affirmations,' the central section of the central prayer in the Rosh Hashana liturgy.[8] The location of this text is significant enough – between the *Malchuyot*, the 'Kingship-Affirmations,' that bear witness to God's kingship from the beginning, and the *Shofarot*, the 'Redemption-Affirmations', that bear witness to the universal acceptance of it in the end. Jews exist, as it were, *between* these two termini, attempting to survive in faithfulness: and rare indeed has been the age in which Jewish survival was possible without steadfast faith in the divine memory. In the *Zichronot* proof-text is heaped upon proof-text to bear this out, and these are followed by the triumphant – or is it near-desperate? – affirmation that 'before the throne of divine glory there is no forgetting'.

Did God remember, then, in all those many years of

Egyptian slavery? Prudently, Rashi refrains from commenting on Exodus 2:24. His prudence contrasts with the stance of Nahmanides who explains that, having lapsed into Egyptian idolatry, the Israelites did not deserve divine memory; that, when at last God did redeem them, it was not for their sake, but for that of His own name. Calling to mind that the slaves included the children, this 'generation' may well feel that Nahmanides adds insult to injury.

Nahmanides does not write in this vein on his own. He relies on Biblical authority – none other than that of Ezekiel. The most 'theocentric' of them all, this prophet begins what may be the sternest of his numerous stern messages with God's refusal to be enquired of by mere humans, and proceeds with a catalogue of Israel's infidelities, harking back to what we have described as the very beginning of Jewish history. They were unfaithful even in Egypt, he asserts. The sufferings of their slavery were deserved, he goes on to say. And the climax of this particular oration is that it was only for His own name's sake that God eventually brought the Israelites forth from Egypt. A theocentric prophet indeed. (Ezekiel 20:3 ff.)[9]

Taking his cue from Ezekiel, one wonders whether Nahmanides would have said what he did on his own, for he also cites a Midrash in which Pharao, in a vain attempt to be cured of leprosy, was in the habit of bathing in the blood of Jewish children.

We have cited from the start an Ezekiel passage: its context remains yet to be given. It was because they had defiled the Land that God had sent His people into exile. It was because they, even in exile, continued to profane His name that the exile was prolonged. And if – as that passage on that wall states – He will gather His people from the nations and return them to their Land, it will only be out of pity for His own holy name and in order to sanctify it. (Ezekiel 36:17-24.) The 'theocentric' prophet, then, is theocentric throughout. The inscription on that wall in *Beit ha-Nassi*, however, makes no reference to its theocentric context.

Nor, for Jews of this 'generation,' can it be otherwise.

Nahmanides may be the profoundest of traditional commentators. Rashi is the most popular and beloved. He too cites that
Midrash about the blood of the children. (Indeed, Nahmanides
cites it on Rashi's authority.) Is it theological prudence alone,
then, that silences him on the subject of divine memory, revived
only after four hundred years of slavery? Citing as he does the
Midrash of the blood of the children, might it be also religious
pain?

Rashi remembers the blood of the Jewish children. Jews,
from this 'generation' onward, dare not forget it. Their memory,
however, is of a different order than Rashi's could have been.
The Midrashic Pharaoh sheds blood for a purpose, the hope to
be cured of leprosy. For the enemy of our time – sleepless, slumberless and no mere Pharaoh – if children were Jewish, the
shedding of blood was *the* purpose – in the end, the only purpose
that remained. Looking for help to commentators, then, this
Jewish 'generation' ought to find Rashi's silence more eloquent
than Nahmanides' words – and also more profound.

But what use are silent commentators? We have no choice
but to go from Rashi back to the 'naked' text – that passage of
it which, to some, marks a 'turning point' in Jewish history and,
to others, the very beginning of it. This, however, leaves us with
nothing but the Ta'nach's own incredibly bold, incredibly sub-
lime anthropomorphism: after four centuries of unspeakable
misery – centuries to which, to be sure, meaning is ascribed by
all-too-pious commentators, but not by the text itself – 'God
remembered'.

## 3  The Jewish Bible: history sacred and plain

Within the Christian Bible, the Old Testament is sacred history
and nothing else. It could hardly be otherwise without provok-
ing complaints such as that of the young Hegel, to the effect that
if his nation needs a history – or pre-history or mythology – it is
its own, not that of an alien nation, imposed on it.[10] In contrast,
the Jewish Ta'nach is not sacred history only – what the
theologians call *Heilsgeschichte*. Much of it is *Geschichte* plain

and simple, to which no higher – saving, divine – purpose is ascribed.

Christians sacralise the Jewish Bible. In ways of its own, Jewish tradition does the same – with history not only in the Bible but also beyond:

> We thank Thee for the miracles, for the liberation, for the mighty acts, for the victories, and for the wars which Thou hast waged for our ancestors in those days on this occasion.

This traditional prayer is reserved for Purim (which celebrates how Haman's plot came to naught) and Hanuka (which celebrates how the Syrian invaders were expelled from the Jerusalem Temple and the Temple service was restored). However, in Esther that tells the Haman-story God is not so much as mentioned, and Maccabees I is an account, not of divine miracles, but of the valour of Jewish soldiers.

Jewish sacralising of the Jewish Bible begins in the Bible itself. In the story of Saul as recorded in Samuel I, God takes away the kingship from Saul for his sin of disobedience. (Samuel 15.) Yet thereafter the book makes no further mention of Saul's sin – this one or others – nor of any further divine punishment, and it ends with Saul taking his own life after a lost battle, a tragic hero mourned by the people. The account of the same events in Chronicles I ends differently. Sin is heaped on sin, and punishment on punishment, the latter ending with Saul's death. In Samuel 'valiant men' travel all night through Philistine-infested land to retrieve the desecrated bodies of Saul and his three sons so as to give them a decent burial, fasting thereafter for seven days. (Samuel 31:8-13.) The account in Chronicles ends as follows:

> So Saul died for his transgression which he committed against the Lord, because of the word of the Lord which he kept not; and also for that he asked counsel of a ghost, to inquire thereby, and inquired not of the Lord; therefore He slew him, and turned the kingdom unto David the son of Jesse. (Chronicles I 10:13-14.)

By this standard David, too, hardly sinless, should have had the kingship taken from him, as well as his life.

Another, deeper look at this sacralising of the Jewish Bible in the Bible itself explains the Chronicler's point of view. Like Samuel I, Kings II ends with history plain and simple which, in both cases (to employ Rosenzweig's expression) is 'murder and manslaughter'. In Kings, Zedekiah, the last reigning king of Judah, 'did that which was evil in the sight of the Lord', causing His anger against Jerusalem and Judah. (II Kings 24:19-20.) But, as regards sins, Zedekiah does not differ from previous kings, and Kings makes no further reference to either the last king's sins or his punishment: the grim events are simply related. Zedekiah rebels against Babylon, and Nebuchadnezzar invades Judah. There ensue the siege and capture of Jerusalem; the burning of the Temple; the apprehension of the fleeing Zedekiah and the slaying of his sons before his eyes, while he himself is carried in chains to Babylon. The book ends – as does so much *Geschichte* that is not *Heilsgeschichte* – on a paltry, if tragic, note. The victorious Chaldeans set up Gedalyah as a puppet regent of the conquered land. Jewish resistance fighters assassinate Gedalyah but have to flee to Egypt in fear of Chaldean vengeance. As for Jehoiachin, a king of Judah no longer reigning, he is released by a Chaldean ruler from a prison in which he has languished for thirty-seven years, to spend the rest of his ignominious life on a pension given him by Chaldean magnanimity.

Quite different is the account of the same events in Chronicles. Zedekiah's sins are spelled out in detail. So is the divine punishment, as well as the fact that it was prophesied by Jeremiah. (II Chronicles 36:11-17, 21.) However, the book (and thus Chronicles as a whole) ends with a quite other prophecy of Jeremiah fulfilled. If Kings ends on a paltry, if tragic, note, Chronicles ends on a note of triumph. Jeremiah's prophecy of divine punishment has come true: so, however, has his promise of divine salvation. The Persian King Cyrus has destroyed wicked Babylon. He now proclaims that God has charged him to build Him a House in Jerusalem, and bids the Jewish exiles to 'go up' to the Land and rebuild it.

> Whosoever there is among you of all His people – the Lord his God be with you – let him go up. (Chronicles II 36:23.)

Thus ends Chronicles. Thus also ends the Jewish Bible. The author of Chronicles 'was attemping to interpret to the restored community in Jerusalem the history of Israel as an eternal covenant between God and David which demanded an obedient response to the divine law.'[11] This was the purpose also of whoever made the Jewish Bible into a sacred canon.

But to Jews of this 'generation' Samuel and Kings speak more loudly than Chronicles. Moreover, even back in 1926 the 'Man' of that 'Today' was told by a mentor (who in many though not all respects is still ours) that, whatever it was that could make the 'many books' into 'one Book' for him, it was not the ancient action that had made the Book into a sacred canon.[12]

## 4    **Esther**

By the standards of canonisers both Christian and Jewish, there are some 'strange books' in the Jewish Bible. Surely the strangest is Esther. Luther had his difficulties with the book. Some Christians go so far as to recommend its expulsion from their Scripture, and not too long ago a Jewish thinker suggested the same. Jewish tradition (as already indicated) sacralises the book, making God into the miraculous Saviour. In the text itself, however, there is no mention of God and – as already shown and to be shown again and again – for better but also for worse this Jewish 'generation' has no choice but to confront the 'naked' Biblical text.[13]

The absence of God is not the only fact that makes Esther a strange book in the sacred Biblical canon. Mordecai is no prophet or martyr but a leader of his people who shows no special religious qualities. Esther is a beautiful Jewish girl who marries out of the faith, and becomes a heroine only because – after hesitating! – she decides to risk her life for her people. These facts, added to the absence of God, make the book alive for secular Jews. What makes it explosively alive for this whole Jewish 'generation', – the 'religious' as well as the 'nonreligious' part of it – is the figure of Haman. Jews seek a Biblical prototype of their worst enemy of all time. Though foredoomed to failure

– Hitler is without precedent – inevitably the search goes on, must go on. It fails with the Pharaohs, for these were pragmatic enemies only, whether motivated by the need for slaves, or by the fear that in wartime the Israelites might join the enemy. (Even the Midrashic Pharaoh is a mere pragmatist, motivated not by thirst for Jewish blood, but by the belief that it will cure his leprosy.) Failing with Pharaoh, the search then turns to Amalek, but this too fails, for this Biblical enemy attacks the weakest only because they are easiest to defeat. The enemy of our time has only one Biblical type that comes close to being his prototype, but this one is uncannily close: the Haman of Esther, who wants to kill all Jews because of the trifling slight of a single Jew. Just so, Hitler is said by some to have murdered six million Jews because – so he may have imagined – his mother was killed, not by cancer, but by the Jewish doctor who, pretending to give her morphine to relieve her pain, in fact poisoned her. Poison was Hitler's favourite method of murdering Jews.[14]

This would suffice to make Esther, once a 'strange' book in the Jewish Bible, strange no more for this Jewish 'generation'. But there is more – much more. In the book Mordecai tells a hesitant Esther that, in case she turns a deaf ear to his plea, deliverance will come to her people 'from another place'. (Esther 4:14.) Traditionally this is an allusion to the unmentioned God. But what if the Biblical Mordecai hoped for no more than some lucky coincidence? The British are said always to muddle through. What if the Mordecai of the 'naked text' means no more than this, that just as luck has always saved the Jewish people, so it will not fail in the present emergency? Esther is a literary masterpiece: what makes it so is the weaving together, with supreme economy, of a series of small coincidences into one large fortunate coincidence. What if Vashti had not been the first militant feminist in history? What if Ahasverus had married a nice Gentile girl? What if Mordecai had not overheard the two who conspired to kill the king? What if the king had not been sleepless that particular night? If any of these 'what ifs' had occurred, Haman would not have failed.

Denuded of pious interpretations, then, the 'naked' Esther

adds up to a lesson in monumental good luck – a lesson supremely relevant, supremely painful, for a Jewish 'generation' after a time of monumental bad luck. This is a theme so haunting that it will be necessary to return to it.[15] For the present this must suffice: during the Holocaust there were thousands of nameless Esthers, less hesitant than the Biblical one to risk their lives for their people: not one had the chance. The much-maligned *Judenraete* included countless would-be Mordecais: to none came the help from another place that would have made him an actual Mordecai. A heroism dwarfing the Biblical – but, unlike the Biblical, doomed to be unsung – was shown by a people, itself doomed to extermination. Yet not one of the saving 'what ifs' occurred. One ponders the minds of the criminals and wonders: is there any better way of understanding them than as zealous readers of Esther, their zeal motivated by the wish to destroy its lesson forever?[16]

This Jewish 'generation' is thus required to face up to a radical question regarding its Ta'nach as a whole. Once the Chronicler's standpoint had caused him to make the Book one by making it into a sacred canon. A possibility no longer open for the modern 'Man of Today' of 1926, he was advised by Martin Buber to find its unity of the book in 'encounters' reflected by it, between 'a group of men and the Lord of the world'. Within the second as much as the first understanding, the 'naked' Esther was a 'strange' book in the one Book.

After what has happened between 1926 and now, however, Esther is strange no more. What if this once-strange book in the Jewish Bible had to be moved from the periphery to the centre, so as to provide the new principle uniting the whole? What if what once had been the repository of divine Revelation had now to become the classic repository of Jewish mythology, that is, for the Jews what the Homeric epics have been, all along, for the Greeks?[17]

## 5    The Homeric epics and the Jewish Bible

There are striking similarities between the Homeric epics among the Greeks and the Jewish Bible among the Jews. Both are literary classics, harking back to the very origins of two peoples that have left a permanent mark on civilisation. Prominent in both is the theme of the human in its relation to the Divine. Even the literary problems are similar, with questions to be raised about written and oral sources and, of course, elusive redactors.

For those holding fast to a revealed canon – the Ta'nach of Jews or the Old Testament of Christians – similarities such as these are of no account: to them, what matters are only the differences. Yet even those dismissing revealed canons – indeed, the very ideas not only of canonicity but also of Revelation – must be struck by a startling difference between Homer and the Jewish Bible: *there is a Greek as well as a Jewish Diaspora: but no Greek ever returned from America to Greece on account of the Iliad or the Odyssey.*

Of this difference one must give an account. To approach the texts with presupposed notions – demythologisation, deconstruction, and so forth – may be fashionable, but can produce few unexpected results: the beginning, at least, must be with texts themselves. Zeus has a flesh-and-blood son, Sarpedon, but not even he, the most powerful god, can save him from death in battle for, as his shrewish wife Hera lectures at him, his death is decreed by Fate. Again, Athene and Ares, the one siding with the Greeks, the other with the Trojans, fight each other, thus robbing themselves of the serenity due to the gods; hence in due course they withdraw from the battle, abandoning their protégés and, with them, human history as a whole. The Homeric gods, then, are either overwhelmed by history or retire from it, letting it run its course. In contrast, the God of the Jewish Bible remains Lord of history from beginning to end. Large parts of the Book may not be *Heilsgeschichte* but mere *Geschichte*, and in the 'strange' Esther God is not so much as mentioned. But even that book – as well as other Biblical books hardly less 'strange' – never denies divine control of history outright – the history of Persians no less than that of Jews. Homer's gods, then, do not wait for a Plato and Aristotle to be – the fashionable term now becomes appropriate – demythologised: the process begins in his epics themselves. But there is no hint of a corresponding process in the Jewish Bible.

The God of Israel resists demythologisation also in subsequent generations. What Homer himself fails to do to his gods is done to them, in the sphere of philosophical thought, by Plato and Aristotle and, in that of political life, by the Roman empire. As Hegel puts it, in the Roman pantheon the gods are all assembled – and all destroyed, to be replaced by Roman emperor-gods.[18] The Jews, in contrast, would do all in their power to prevent their God's presence in the Roman pantheon – and fight if necessary unto death rather than accept the statue of Caligula in the Jerusalem Temple.[19] So it was in the sphere of political life. As for the sphere of philosophical thought, Maimonides loved Aristotle; but his God remained the Creator of the world.[20]

This was the state of Jewish affairs through the Middle Ages. With the advent of modern secularism, indiscriminate demythologising of past gods became a widespread procedure, and what was done to gods-in-general was done to the God-of-Israel-in-particular when modern critics chopped up the Jewish Bible into J, E, D, P, R and so forth, each of these 'sources' having God-ideas but none God Himself. One contemplates this powerful, increasingly world-wide sweep of modern demythologising of past gods – this world-wide secularisation – and asks: the work of Hegel and Kierkegaard, of Rosenzweig and Buber – was all this not futile? Was Buber's great essay of 1926 not, after all, a mere rearguard battle, with its central claim that the 'Man' of its 'Today', if reading the Jewish Bible, could not, to be sure, believe apriori, but also need not disbelieve a priori?

The question and the doubt existed in 1926. For a Jewish 'generation' over half a century later, they have or should have become monumental and inescapable. Attacks on the Jewish Bible by Marx, Nietzsche and sundry lesser critics have or should have become trivial, even picayune, compared to what was done to the Book and its God by events. So it is for those who read Esther – thus we have argued – as after the Holocaust it must be read. So it is also for those who, having read Esther in this perspective, look yet again at that Ezekiel passage on that wall in Jerusalem. Could it be, is the question as one stares at those words once more, that the God of Israel and His promise to Israel, after all, are a myth which, like all myth, requires demythologisation; but that the myth needed to be believed by exiled Jews if they were to survive exile? What if all the Old Testament demythologising, done by scholars and theologians for several centuries, were trifling compared to the *real* demythologisation of the Ta'nach, done in our time *by Jews themselves*, with their collective decision to stop relying on others, human or divine; with the collective Jewish decision to take the collective Jewish secular courage in its collective hands: with the act of ending Jewish exile by 'going up' to the Land?

Is this, then, the *real* act that has made the Ta'nach, at long last, for the Jews what the Homeric epics have been for the Greeks all along? Is this the true, the final meaning of that Ezekiel passage as inscribed on that wall in our time?

## 6  The death and resurrection of hope

Such was the mood of many at the time when the state was founded. It was captured well by Arthur Koestler, a man of his time. Koestler was involved in all the major causes of the age and therefore also in the Jewish cause, considered tragic by him because of its 'abnormalcy'. In a work published in 1949 he declared that the abnormalcy, and hence the tragedy, had come to an end. The Jewish state should – would – be a state like all the others, its Jews 'abnormal' no more. As for Jews outside it, they now could – should – cease to be Jews and assimilate. To be sure, hitherto such as he had been obliged to remain Jews, this in solidarity with Jews elsewhere, exiled still. However, with Jewish exile now ended, this obligation had itself come to an end. The 1949 book ends as follows: 'The fumes of the death camps still linger over Europe. There must be an end of every Calvary.'[21]

Late in life Koestler had become interested in religion, not, however, in his own religion: his prophecy of the end of Jewish 'abnormalcy' resorts to a Christian symbol.

This was in 1949. Forty years later – a Biblical number!– matters are different. Exiled still, Jews in the unfree world cannot assimilate. In the free world they cannot do so honorably: they owe the old solidarity to Jews still in exile, and a new solidarity to the Jewish state. Contrary to Koestler's expectation, this state is not like others. Contrary to the expectation of anyone, it could not be 'normal' if it wanted to be for, besieged still, it is the one state on earth whose right to exist, even nice people imply, is debatable. Who keeps intoning that Canada or England or Luxemburg has a right to exist? The right to existence of these states – of every other state – is considered self-evident.

'Abnormal' because of enemies without, Israel is unlike other states because of consciousness within. We have considered responses to the Holocaust by religious thinkers: the late 1940s, 1950s and even early 1960s were too soon. 1949 was too soon also for the secularist Arthur Koestler. But even as the events themselves become more remote in time, a Jewish *Erschuetterung* at what they were deepens, and spreads beyond the survivors to the second and third generation; and yet another look at that Ezekiel text inscribed on that wall in Jerusalem calls forth, less and less, Messianic associations and, increasingly, apocalyptic ones.

That inscription is taken from the thirty-sixth chapter of Ezekiel. The chapter immediately following pierces the soul as perhaps no other in the entire Bible, Jewish or Christian. Its subject is death and resurrection. The prophet has a vision of a valley full of dead bones, 'lo, they were very dry'. He is asked whether these bones can live, and he replies – what other reply is possible? – 'O Lord God, Thou knowest'. Then he is bidden to prophecy that these bones will live. And behold – so the vision continues – , a noise, a commotion as the bones come together, as they assume flesh, sinews and, finally, breath. The text goes on:

> Then He said unto me: 'Son of man, these bones are the whole house of Israel. Behold, they say, 'Our bones are dried up, and our hope is lost: we are clean cut off.' Therefore prophecy unto them, 'Thus saith the Lord God: "Behold, I will open your graves, and cause you to come out of your graves, O My people; and I will bring you into the Land of Israel. And ye shall know that I am the Lord . . . " (Ezekiel 37:2,3,9-11.)

Rare is the Biblical text so hard to read 'nakedly' – without commentary. Sober as usual, Rashi takes it to refer to the sufferings of exile and the restoration to the Land – but even he cannot avoid a hint at the resurrection of the dead. On our part, as stressed from the start, we seek no more from this text than further light on that other Ezekiel passage, and on that one only as inscribed at that place in our time.

To visitors – first to Auschwitz or Bergen–Belsen, then to Jerusalem – Ezekiel's image of death and resurrection comes easily to mind. It could come too easily. In Ezekiel's image, the dead have fallen in battle. The dead of the Holocaust were denied battle, its opportunity and its honour. Denied the peace even of bones, they were denied the honour also of graves, for they, the others, ground their bones to dust and threw the dust into rivers. To apply Ezekiel's image of Jewish death to the Holocaust, then, is impossible. The new enemy, no mere Haman, not only succeeded where Haman failed, for he murdered the Jewish people. He murdered also Ezekiel's image of Jewish death.

Murdered as well was the prophet's image of Jewish resurrection. Whether in terms of future, Messianic time or of a world-to-come beyond time, 'Resurrection' connotes redemptive finality. But much though we might yearn to take either recourse, confined as we are to that Ezekiel passage on that wall, we cannot, dare not, ascribe redemptive finality to the State of Israel. For the secular-minded this is in any case impossible. As for the religiously-minded, they most assuredly may believe that this time, like previous times, salvation came

67

to the Jewish people, this time, monumentally with the restoration of the state; yet as at length the Holocaust penetrates the religious no less than the secular consciousness, neither can shut out the awful thought that a salvation that came too late once could come too late again. And even as this post-Holocaust consciousness takes hold within, the state finds itself surrounded without by Syrians, Iraqis, Libyans, Algerians, Iranians and the rest of an immense multitude, more 'gigantic' than the 'giants,' feared by ten of the twelve Biblical spies, ever were. Back in Biblical origins, hope carried the fearful people, nevertheless, to the Land. Clearly, only a hope without precedent keeps them in the Land today.

Then what remains of Ezekiel's image of Jewish death and resurrection? Nothing but this: hope. But how? In the prophet's vision, the House of Israel, its bones dried up, lament *avda tikvatenu*, 'our hope is lost.' The Zionist anthem, now Israel's national anthem, contains the words *lo avda tikvatenu*, 'our hope is not lost'. Its author, the Hebrew poet Naftali Herz Imber (1856-1909), had Ezekiel in mind when he contradicted the despair of the 'bones'. But neither he nor subsequent Zionist generations could have imagined the significance this contradiction would one day assume. One ponders this hymn as it is sung now. One looks for a parallel but finds none. One listens to one's friends and neighbours as they sing the words, and wonders whether they understand. As one sings them oneself, one hardly knows how this singing is possible. 'Our hope is lost,' is the lament of Ezekiel's bones, of the house of Israel. This lament proved true in the Holocaust beyond the limits of the previous imagination. 'Abandon hope,' are the words greeting those entering Dante's hell. Even so it cannot touch the innocent. The Holocaust-world touched *none but* the innocent. What is innocent if not birth? Who is innocent if not children? When the children were thrown into the Auschwitz flames hell was surpassed. When their screams could be heard in the camp hope was murdered. It was murdered for the little ones. It was murdered also for those hearing their screams. And as we re-hear these screams it is murdered again.

Hope might have survived during the Holocaust on one condition. Having recourse to the Talmud, the 'Malbim' *ad locum* holds a view but weakly supported by the 'naked' text – that Job was not given new children in place of the old, that his first children were resurrected.[22] This was prior to the Holocaust. During the Holocaust, the Budapest Rabbi Yissachar Shlomo Teichthal, a leading Hasid of the Munkacher Rebbe, hoped that, for the remnant to 'rise and ascend to Zion' would be to 'reconstruct' the murdered people, that it would 'bring about their rebirth'.[23] But Teichthal's hope for the Messianic End remained unfulfilled – as unsupported in life as the 'Malbim's' reading of Job by the Biblical text. Hope, then, did not survive, even if it was 'last to die'.[24] Then what is this Jewish 'generation' doing when, contradicting Ezekiel's 'bones', *lo avda tikvatenu* is sung? Jewish hope was born when Abram (not Abraham yet) heeded the call to get out of his country, from his kindred, from his father's house, unto the Land God would show him. This is if we follow the tradition. If we follow the scholars and Genesis is myth, hope was born with the 'turning point' of the Exodus. Hope went on living through the millennia, and thus there were Jewish children. When at length Jewish hope was murdered in the Holocaust, Jews coming after might have thrown away the Jewish Book, might have ended Jewish history, might have – this above all – remained childless. This decision would have been reasonable, for without hope Jews cannot live. When, contradicting this reasonableness, Jews instead opened a new page in their history – restored a Jewish state – a unique intertwining of religious faith and secular courage – *they resurrected the murdered hope. The resurrected hope, and it alone, is what remains of Ezekiel's image of death and resurrection.*

But a resurrected hope is not like a hope that never died. Murdered once, this hope could be murdered again. Hence, as a new page is being written in the age-old history that is between the people and its Book, those engaged in the writing of it – 'religious' and 'secular' Jews – are united by a hope resurrected but shot through with doubt, the ones hoping, the others acting as though they were hoping, that – after twelve years that were equal, not to a mere four hundred but to a thousand – 'God remembered'.

# The children of Rachel, of Haman, of Job: post-Holocaust possibilities of a fraternal Jewish-Christian reading of the Book belonging to both

## 1    Too late – and too soon

In 1963 Karl Barth came to the United States for his only visit. There he asked for a meeting with a dozen or so German-speaking Jewish theologians, and those invited, myself included, were glad to accept: we remembered his anti-Nazi record, and were awed by his theological achievement. Present on the Christian side were, with Barth himself, his two sons, theologians both, and the meeting, held in Chicago, was marked by the friendliest of spirits. Yet as a Jewish–Christian dialogue it was a failure.

Not that Barth did not try to make it a success, and this with his opening proposal. In his 1942 'Israel and the Church' he had theologised *about* Jews, 'self-evidently'[1] as a New-Testa-ment-Church witness. Now, two decades later, he wished to speak *with* Jews. In effect if not those actual words, then, he proposed that we, Christians and Jews, so to speak leave at home our hermeneutical armature, the ones their New Testa-ment, the others their rabbinic sources, and engage in a frater-nal reading the Book that belongs to us both. Against the back-ground of Barth's entire theological career, the proposal was revolutionary.

It came too soon for us Jews. One (who had delved into the Church Dogmatics in some detail) rejoined that Barth should study Talmud with us, as if Barth had not just suggested suspending his own New Testament. As for the rest, though awed by Barth's theology, we knew it too little in depth to grasp the radicalism of his proposal.

For Barth himself, his own suggestion came too late. How in its light he would have had to re-write his 'Israel and the Church', and indeed the Church Dogmatics as a whole; whether the whole vast edifice could have survived at all: all this cannot be known. Known is only this, that after his return from America he did not go on with his work, that the Church Dogmatics remained incomplete.[2]

That 1963 was too soon, still, for Jews and Christians alike, emerged in our three-hour-or-so meeting. To my recollection neither the Holocaust nor Israel was ever mentioned, or if so only in passing, and not as of any theological significance.

A quarter of a century later, most of the evidence indicates that it is too soon, still, for a post-Holocaust theology worthy of the name – indeed, for settling whether such a thing is possible. But is it too soon for reviving Barth's 1963 proposal? The Roman Catholic theologian David Tracy has called for a hermeneutic of suspicion as well as retrieval, without exempting the New Testament from the suspicion.[3] The Protestant theologian Roy Eckardt has defined Christian theology as 'Jewish theology done by Christians', while his colleague Franklin Littell has called for a 'Reformation' in the churches more radical and universal than the sixteenth-century event known by that name.[4] Is the 'Aryan'/'non-Aryan' abyss, then, first legislated in 1935, at last beginning to penetrate the Christian theological consciousness?

'Reformation' turns the mind to the country of the Reformation – and of the 'Aryan'/'non-Aryan' abyss. In 1939 I had fled from Germany, the land of my birth. In 1983 I returned, not for my first but for my first theological visit. There the Roman Catholic theologian Hanns-Hermann Henrix affirmed that Christian anti-Judaism will not end until Christians find a positive relation to Jews, not despite their non-acceptance of the Christ but because of it. On his part, Martin Stoehr, a Protestant, spelled out the following: 'We Christians have lived alongside Jews for nearly two millennia. But we have never listened to them, and our Christian faith has not helped us in this regard. Then why do we want to listen to them now? Not because of our Christian faith, but because six million Jews were murdered.' He ended his major address as follows: 'We Christians must begin all over again, with the first two questions of the Bible. "Where are you, Man?" and "Where is your brother?"' Events have revolutionised the thinking of these two German theologians, one Roman Catholic, the other Protestant. No longer able to begin with a New Testament superseding the Old, they begin once more with the beginning – an 'Old' Testament as old-new for them as the Ta'nach has been for Jews all along. In this, we learn from Eberhard Bethge, they had a precursor in Dietrich Bonhoeffer.

## 2   The lament of Rachel and the new covenant

In North America, if not Poland or the Vatican, Jewish–Christian dialogue is easy and popular. It could be too easy, too popular. Much has been achieved since the days when, Brotherhood Week being over and done with, both Jews and Christians would return to their theological sleep. Dialogue has made once-taboo subjects, such as New Testament antisemitism and 'Grace' in Old Testament 'Law', taboo no more. Yet a real breakthrough requires the shared reading, not of texts that join Jews and Christians together – Creation, the Ten Commandments or even texts about Law and Grace – but of such as set them starkly apart.

> Thus saith the Lord:
> 'A voice is heard in Ramah
> Lamentation, and bitter weeping,
> Rachel weeping for her children;
> She refuseth to be comforted for her children,
> Because they are not.'
> Thus saith the Lord:
> 'Refrain thy voice from weeping,
> And thine eyes from tears;
> For thy work shall be rewarded,
> Saith the Lord;

> And they shall come back from the land of the enemy.'
> (Jeremiah 31:15-16.)

> Behold, the days come, saith the Lord, that I will make a new
> covenant with the house of Israel, and with the house of Judah;
> not according to the covenant that I made with their fathers in
> the day that I took them by the hand to bring them out of the land
> of Egypt; forasmuch as they broke My covenant, although I was
> Lord over then, saith the Lord. But this is the covenant that I will
> make with the house of Israel after those days, saith the Lord, I
> will put My law in their inward parts, and in their hearts will I
> write it; and I will be their God, and they shall be My people; and
> they shall teach no more every man his neighbour, and every
> man his brother, saying, 'Know the Lord'; for they shall all know
> Me, from the least of them unto the greatest of them, saith the
> Lord . . . (Jeremiah 31:31-4.)

Few Biblical chapters set Jews and Christians as clearly apart as
this one in Jeremiah. No Christian can dispense with its new
covenant promise; no Jew, with its promise to Rachel. Moreover, as Jews and Christians today attempt to share these two
texts in this chapter, there is a *novum*. Never merely peripheral
for Jews, the weeping Rachel has moved into the centre – and
no shared Jewish–Christian reading is possible unless she
moves into the Christian centre also: a Rachel weeping for
children who have not returned, nor ever will return, from the
land of the enemy.

## 3   The 'naked' text as threat

The advent of Nazism was followed by a renaissance of Judaism
in Germany. Of this, part was the *Philo Lexikon*, first published
in November 1934, a one-volume 'Handbook of Jewish Knowledge' for those many German Jews who lacked all Jewish
knowledge but were in dire need of it now. Its brief article on
Martin Luther states that his *Von den Juden und ihren Luegen*
('Of the Jews and Their Lies') has lost its former relevance.

Exactly four years later this statement was refuted. In 1542
Luther had demanded that synagogues be burned to the ground;

on 9 November 1938 it was done. In his pamphlet the father of the Reformation had advised that Jews be robbed of their property and forced into physical labour; this advice too was followed to the letter during and after the so-called *Kristallnacht*, when Jewish stores were smashed and looted, and thousands of Jewish males (this writer included) were carted off to concentration camps for just this, forced physical labour. The Jewish response to the events of 1933 had been a great, now nearly forgotten, flowering of spirit. In a single night just over five years later, all this was brutally destroyed.

Luther was neither the first nor the last great exponent of Christian love to hate Jews. His case is special because he opened a new page in Christian history, and because, some twenty years earlier, he had expressed pro-Jewish sentiments such as 'Jews had not heard in a thousand years'.[5] Most noteworthy of all is this: the man who came to hate Jews loved the Jewish Bible, so deeply as to produce a German translation that is a classic still.

Conventional wisdom has it that the outpourings of the old Luther are those of a frustrated missionary-to-the-Jews. Were this the whole cause of his hatred, the *Philo Lexikon* would have been right in considering his 1542 pamphlet as no longer relevant. In Nazi Germany, what Lutheran – or Christian of *any* kind – wanted to convert Jews? Even Christians in the forefront of the anti-Nazi struggle had trouble just barely tolerating 'non-Aryan' Christians, that is, Jews already converted.[6] Then why was the *Philo Lexikon* wrong?

For Luther the 'Word and Grace of God' are a 'downpour'. The experience of it is the heart and soul of his faith. It reaches him through his New Testament, but just as surely also through his Old. Yet he finds it necessary to write: 'Know ye that the Word and Grace of God is a downpour which moves from place to place, never to return where it once was. It was once with the Jews. But what is gone is gone. *Now the Jews have nothing*. [Italics added.]'[7]

These are the words of a disturbed man. He protests – too much. The Old Testament which inspires his love also inspires a fear – that if, God forbid, the 'downpour' should be with the Jews still, it might shut him out. The old Luther, then, hates Jews not despite his love of the Jewish Bible but because of it. This ought to disturb Christians today.

One suggestion never entered either Luther's diatribe or his mind: extermination. This was not because of Christian love for Jews – he showed none – but because of his hope for their eventual conversion. He derived this from the Bible he loved – both Old Testament and New. This love was not shared by Hitler's Germany. Having acted on Luther's advice in 1938, that Germany soon went further. Of its weak feelings for the New Testament the ludicrous 'German Christians' with their ludicrous 'Aryan' Christ are sufficient proof. The Old Testament, in contrast, filled Hitler's Germany with hatred. The very first treatise that bears the future Führer's name manages to make Moses into a bolshevist, Lenin into a Jew, and the Jewish Bible into the oldest record of all evil.[8] As for *Mein Kampf*, its message is little but this, that 'Aryans' are the chosen people, without a God, to be sure, to do any choosing. Yet neither its own 700 pages nor the Reich's subsequent thinkers ever managed to define 'Aryan' except as 'not-non-Aryan' – and that was the Jew. Such was the *Weltanschauung*. Its truth would not be fully verified – that is, *made true* – until the last Jew was dead. Museums for an 'extinct race' were already planned. And when the Thousand-Year-Reich came crashing down before the millennium of a *judenrein* world was attained, the Führer's last will and testament made further pursuit of it obligatory for future 'Aryan' generations.

Historians have failed to explain the 'why' of the Holocaust. They will surely never wholly succeed. They will fail entirely, however, unless they grasp that Hitler, Streicher, and the unknown SS man who was a mass-murderer not merely hated the Old Testament: they also feared it.

This ought to shock Jews-and-Christians-in-dialogue out of the near-slumber of all-too-amiable dialogues. Luther loved the Jewish Bible; Hitler hated it; yet the two had this in common: the Book was a threat to both.

The shock can only be salutary. Jews may love Christian company in reading their Ta'nach: they have reason also to fear it. As for Christians, if that no more and hence Gentiles, they may view the Jewish Book as the epic of an alien people; or else, if Christians still, they may continue to claim it as their Old Testament. In either case they dare not read the Book with Jewish friends today – nay, by themselves! – without ridding themselves of the fear of the Book. In the first case, this requires the making of aliens into friends; in the second, it requires Christian auto-emancipation from every trace of the need to rob Jews of their Ta'nach, in the process of claiming it as their own Old Testament.

## 4    Hegel on Job – a necessary prolepsis

These two possibilities, for our time, were both explored by Hegel in his time.

'Is Judaea, then, the Teuton's fatherland?', Hegel asks in an early manuscript. A trend was just beginning that would reach a high point, but not its climax, with Richard Wagner: the 'Teuton' was to find his 'fatherland' in the myths of ancient Germany. Hegel, though too young and unsure of his views to publish his manuscript, is untempted. Nor is he tempted by the gods of 'Achaea' – these he loved – , for these can be resurrected no more than those of ancient Germany. 'The only book of antiquity still in living use' – thus Franz Rosenzweig was to refer to the Torah, well over a century after Hegel's question. Well over a century earlier, Hegel makes no such statement, nor can he. Yet because 'paganism' is 'conquered' by 'Christianity' his question is serious and, to him, troubling.

His answer is negative – necessarily so, for the Old Testament contains the mythology of an alien people, and the 'fatherland' Hegel's 'Teuton' of 1785 seeks is his own: the young Hegel is not a Christian. Hegel's necessary negativity then and there, however, does not necessitate hostility, here and now. A non-Christian Hegel today might read the Jewish book fraternally, say, with an Israeli friend, for one is not threatened by the mythology of a people other than one's own.

So much for the young Hegel.[9] The mature Hegel is neither a non-Christian nor a Christian: he is a post-Christian. From Paul to the present, Christians have affirmed their Christian truth against all other religions – pagan, Muslim, Jewish. (Indeed, much present Christian 'outreach' for 'dialogue' continues to be suspect, and is suspected.) On his part, Hegel is post-Christian in that, on the one hand, his Christianity is the 'absolute' religion, superseding the relative truths of every other religion; yet in that, on the other hand, it must be given the 'form' of a 'thought' that does justice to all religions, each on its own terms and in its own right. This requires Hegel's own mature thought to do justice to Judaism.[10]

This was then and there. Here and now, would Hegel's 'absolute religion' be possible? Europe is the world's centre no more, nor is central Europe the centre's centre. Buber's 'Man' of 1926 is gone. So is Hegel's 'absolute religion' of a century earlier. In our 'here and now', Hegel would surely persist in his mediating activity, of pluralities and, so far as possible, of conflicts and fragmentation. (He might emerge as a deeper philosopher of pluralism and dialogue than has yet appeared.) But recourse from present realities – pluralism, conflict, fragmentation – to a 'higher synthesis' – his one-time 'absolute religion' – would require a turn of thought on his part contrary to its deepest, life-long commitment: flight from the 'actual world'.

This might be here and now. Then and there, evidently Hegel can do no complete justice to Judaism, for his 'absolute religion' is Christian, and of Judaism he knows only his own Old Testament. The partial justice to Judaism that, nevertheless, he does is outside our present scope.[11] Well within it is only his Job, perceived by him as the Jew *in extremis*, hence as the Jew *par excellence*. This Job he perceives, too, as being no mere anachronism: indeed, in some respects he represents the human condition as a whole.[12]

Let us compare Hegel's Job with its counterpart in Rudolf Otto. A protesting Job has upheld his innocence against the theology of his friends: this much is obvious and universally agreed. For *The Idea of the Holy* everything climaxes in what happens when Job is confronted, no longer with arguments by theologians but, in the whirlwind, with nothing less than the Divine Presence. This may do nothing to justify Job's suffering and hence to dissolve his protest. Yet such is the 'mystical', 'numinous' Presence of the 'Holy' as to make Job respond:

> Behold, I am of small account;
> What shall I answer Thee?
> I lay my hand upon my mouth.
> Once have I spoken, but I will not answer again;
> Yea, twice, but I will proceed no further. (Job 40:4-5.)

To Otto, this response to the Divine Presence is everything; to sundry modern-leftist critics, nothing. In their eyes, Job either protests to the end – chapters 38-40 of the book, culminating in the passage just cited, are pious additions by fraudulent priests – , or else would protest to the end were he a better, braver Job, i.e., a modern leftist atheist. Unlike Otto, the critics have no sense of the divine Presence.

The recovery of this sense has made *The Idea of the Holy* a twentieth-century classic. Having recovered that sense, Otto perceives the 'guiltless suffering of the righteous' as 'the most mystical of all problems of the Old Covenant', and Job's self-surrender to the Divine Presence as its 'solution'. This, he goes on to assert, is a 'prophecy of Golgotha', where 'the solution of the problem, already adumbrated in Job, is repeated and surpassed'. Otto's Job, then, is a proto-Christian, rendered anachronistic by the Christ; and this he is because, already 'rehabilitated' by the Divine Presence and his own surrender, he does not need the eventual restoration of his former good fortune that causes him to die 'old and full of days'. (Job 42:17.) This, his new seven sons and three daughters included, is merely 'an extra payment thrown in after quittance has already been rendered'.[13]

The leftist critics have no sense of the Divine Presence. Hegel does. Yet his Job is neither a proto-Christian nor rendered anachronistic by the Christ. Like Otto's, his Job 'renounces' everything, his innocence, his protest, his very self. Yet – a dialectical notion beyond Otto's ken – in the very act of 'renunciation' he 'renounces renunciation' also: even *in extremis* the supreme display of divine 'Power' is fragmentary unless it turns into a display of 'Justice' also. For Otto's Job, absorbed as he is in his soul, the Divine Presence completes the necessary vindication. For Hegel's Job, his vindication is not complete until 'the Lord blesses his latter end more than his beginning'. (Job 42:12.)

This Job is closer to that of Judaism. Also, he is no anachronism – either in Hegel's nineteenth century or in ours. The greatest man of this century, with his country's fortunes at their lowest ebb and the fate of humanity in the balance, held fast to divine Justice. 'The mills of God grind slowly,' Winston Churchill declared, 'but they grind mighty fine.'

As Hegel understands him, Job is vindicated when 'temporal happiness' is restored to him. This is the expression he uses. He makes no special mention of the children. Not much mention was made of them by commentators through the ages.

## 5    Children of Rachel

To ignore the children, possible with Job, is impossible with the Jeremiah chapter that is our chief text.

Who are Rachel's children?

> Then Herod, when he saw that he was mocked of the wise men, was exceeding wroth, and set forth, and slew all the children that were in Bethlehem, and in all the coasts thereof, from two years old and under . . . Then was fulfilled that which was spoken by Jeremiah the prophet, saying, 'A voice is heard in Ramah, lamentation and bitter weeping, Rachel is weeping for her children, she refuseth to be comforted for her children, for they are not.'
>
> But when Herod was dead, behold, an angel of the Lord appeared in a dream to Joseph in Egypt, saying, 'Arise, and take the young child and his mother, and go to the Land of Israel . . .' (Matthew 2:16-19.)

Without this New Testament passage, the children of Rachel, evidently, are Jews and they alone. With it (and others with the same message), equally evidently, they are Christians and they alone, for in them Jeremiah's prophecy is 'fulfilled'. A fraternal Jewish-Christian reading of the Rachel-text, then, seems impossible both with Matthew and without it.

The difficulty is aggravated when we turn from Jeremiah's Rachel- to its new-covenant-text. This is cited in Hebrews in full, with Paul concluding as follows:

> In that he saith, 'A new covenant,' he hath made the first old. Now that which decayeth and waxeth old is ready to vanish away. (Hebrews 8:13.)

What Paul affirms in Hebrews Augustine confirms in *The City of God*:

> The testimonies of holy scriptures ... must be first of all taken out of the New Testament, and then out of the Old. For though the latter be more ancient, yet the former are more worthy, as being the true contents of the latter. (Book XX, ch. 4.)

Jeremiah's Old Testament 'prophecy', then, is to be read in the light of its New Testament 'fulfilment', and in this alone: this, affirmed by Paul and confirmed by Augustine, is reconfirmed again and again through the Christian ages, right up to Rudolf Bultmann and Karl Barth. No wonder this fact is reflected through these same ages in Jewish commentaries. Neither Rashi nor David Kimchi (1160?–1235) refer to the Christian view of Jeremiah's new-covenant-text. (They have reason not to, for they live in Christian countries.) Yet surely that view is on Rashi's mind when, cautious as always, and though commenting on the new-covenant-passage elsewhere – briefly, innocuously – , he omits any comment *ad locum*. More obviously still is the Christian view on Kimchi's mind when he ends his comment as follows: 'He [i.e. Jeremiah] does not say that they will all be equal in wisdom, for *this is not possible* ... but to 'know Him' is to fear Him and follow in His ways. [Italics added.] Through the ages, then, these texts have inspired Jewish-Christian warfare rather than friendship. Can this yield to a fraternal sharing?

It can, if the 'Reformation' called for – nay, in small ways already initiated – is given a chance. Christians are 'to start all over again, with the first two questions of the Bible . . . ': but this Bible – the Jewish Ta'nach, the Christian Old Testament – is theirs only through the New. They are to 'relate positively to Jews, not in spite but because of their nonacceptance of the Christ': but this is possible only if the New Testament in no sense supersedes the Jewish Ta'nach. The Christian 'Reformation' called for, then, may be called a *destructive recovery* – a process, that is, in which the Christian Bible is recovered, but only as at the same time Christian supersessionism – a bimillennial mistake – is, step by step, done away with, overcome. What Christian understanding of Jeremiah's new-covenant-text will emerge from this process is for Christians themselves to discover. (How might a future Barth re-write – or replace! – the *Church Dogmatics*?) A Jewish response, on its part, overcoming Rashi's and Kimchi's defensiveness, might well understand this text as opening a gate to the Gentiles.

In such a shared reading of Jeremiah, who then are the children of Rachel? They are two kinds. The ones, flesh-and-blood children, are Jews. The others become children of Rachel through the return of one flesh-and-blood Jewish child from exile to the Land of Israel.

We must cite a verse from our Jeremiah chapter not cited hitherto:

> Thus saith the Lord: Sing with gladness for Jacob. And shout at the head of the nations; Announce ye, praise ye and say: O Lord, save Thy people, the remnant of Israel. (Jeremiah 31:7.)

This verse is introduced now because of its notion of remnant, a notion applied here to Jewish existence but appropriated by Paul for Christian existence. Whatever else Jeremiah means – or other prophets invoked by Paul in his own use of the notion – 'remnant' is a flesh-and-blood people, its exile real, geographical. Paul's remnant, in contrast, is a church, constituted by Grace (Romans 9:27, 11:5-6); and 'exile', whether or not over and done with, is not geographical, but a state of soul.[14]

The notion of remnant, then, discloses an existential difference between the two kinds of Rachel's children. It has remained real through the ages. However, not until our age did it become catastrophic enough to alter the condition of both remnants.

## 6    The promise of modern scholarship and its limits

A promise has come on the scene with the advent of modernity. The two sets of Rachel's children, the old and the new, are not the same. Their remnants are not the same. Their situation is not the same. But a detachment is possible from these differences, and through it a stance toward the Jewish Book no less objective than that of a botanist peering through a microscope. Such is the ideal of modern Biblical scholarship. For Jews and Christians seeking a fraternal reading of the Jewish Bible, such is its promise.

A great document of this promise fulfilled is the many-volume Anchor Bible. One New Testament volume is by a Jewish scholar. So are Genesis and Ezekiel, in the Old. The first Isaiah is by a Jew, the second, by a Christian. The Jeremiah volume is the work of a Christian.

Let us test the fulfilled promise with an example. Of the new-covenant-passage the author of the Jeremiah commentary, John Bright, writes as follows: '. . . it represents what might well be considered the high point of his theology. It is certainly one of the profoundest and most moving passages in the entire Bible.' Of the Rachel-passage he has nothing to say.[15]

Bright's statement requires analysis. Even Indian, Chinese or Soviet Biblical scholars might 'consider' the new-covenant-passage the 'high point' of Jeremiah's 'theology'. Eschatological, it is, arguably, pointed to by the prophet's entire career, with his fears and hopes, his denunciations of his people and his tears for them. John Bright, then, makes a scholar's judgement about Jeremiah's theology; he does not insinuate his own.

But to go on, in whose Bible is the new-covenant passage 'one of the profoundest'? In the Jewish Ta'nach the Song at the

Sea (Exodus 15) and the event at Sinai (Exodus 19:18-25, 20:1-14) have greater profundity, and when the Ten Commandments are recited in the Shabbat Torah reading the congregation rises.

To go on from 'most profound' to 'most moving': most moving *for whom*? The Rachel passage Bright ignores. Yet just this is most moving for Jews – or for all who ever wailed, or thought of wailing, at the Wall in Jerusalem, weeping with Rachel for children, exiled still.

At stake in this sample (and others that could be given) is no mere occasional bias, creeping into an otherwise 'value-free' objectivity. At stake is objectivity itself – its scope and its limits. First, equal attention to every Biblical text is impossible: selective attention is inevitable. Second, selectivity by itself implies value-judgements, and one does not avoid these by escaping from the vastness of the Book into minutiae within miniscule parts of it. Most important, third, is that scholarship goes beyond the dating and philology of texts to their understanding, and one scholar's understanding always seems to differ from that of others.

Let us compare the understanding of the new-covenant passage given by two reputable scholars:

*Interpretation A*:

This passage is the 'climax' of Jeremiah's prophecies of salvation, for the new covenant is not a mere renewal of the old. Its essence lies in the 'transformation' of the 'duty to obey' the 'covenantal law' as the 'expression of an alien will' into a 'need felt by the heart itself', with the result that the law loses its 'heterogeneous character'.[16]

*Interpretation B*:
This passage represents the resolution of a 'tension' between the 'moral demand that sets limits to the working of God' and the 'religious demand that subjects all to divine control'. The 'eschatological' resolution will render man 'incapable of sinning'.[17]

We make four observations:
(a) Neither interpreter finds his categories in the text,

which does not know of an 'alien' will or a 'heterogeneous' law, any more than of a 'tension' between a 'moral' and a 'religious' demand. Consciously or unconsciously, these categories are brought to the text.

(b) The categories used by both interpreters are recognisably Kantian.

(c) Despite this fact, the two interpretations not only differ; if pressed, they are incompatible. In the first view, the new covenant may become (if it not already is) a reality, so that the old covenant may become (if it not already is) superseded. (If further proof of this is needed, the first interpreter supplies it in full.)[18] For the second interpreter, the new covenant is an ideal, which as such can be approximated but never be reached, so that the old covenant is not and cannot ever be superseded.

(d) The author of the first interpretation is a Christian, that of the second a Jew.

We ask: do the categories brought to the text by the two interpreters rest on an independent basis, so that it is only, as it were, by happy coincidence that the conclusions reached conform to their religious commitments; or – with such coincidences being past reasonable belief – do these categories, on the contrary, flow from prior, pre-reflective commitments? If the latter, can this 'bias' be removed, or are pre-reflective commitments inescapably part of the human condition, the scholarly included?

The latter view accords with recent hermeneutical theory. Summing up a near-consensus, H. G. Gadamer writes: 'The overcoming of all prejudices, this global demand of the Enlightenment, . . . prove[s] to be itself a prejudice, the removal of which opens a way to an appropriate understanding of our finitude; which dominates not only our humanity but also our historical consciousness.[19] The promise of modern scholarship, then, has limits, surely the greater in the Biblical case, in which pre-reflective commitments – at least Jewish and Christian – are deep, and go back to time immemorial.

As they read the Book that belongs to them both, then, neither the Jewish nor the Christian remnant can detach itself wholly from its existential condition. This fact it is all the more urgent to recognise, ever since that condition was changed, for both remnants, by what happened at Auschwitz and Ravensbrueck.

## 7 The children of Auschwitz and the mothers of Ravensbrueck

A former Polish guard testified at the Nuremberg trials, having sworn to tell the truth and nothing but the truth. This is part of his testimony:

> *Witness*: . . . women carrying children were [always] sent with them to the crematorium. The children were then torn from their parents outside the crematorium and sent to the gas chambers separately. When the extermination of the Jews in the gas chambers was at its height, orders were issued that the children were to be thrown straight into the crematorium furnaces, or into the pit near the crematorium, without being gassed first.
>
> *Smirnov* [Soviet prosecutor]: How am I to understand this? Did they throw them into the fire alive, or did they kill them first?
>
> *Witness*: They threw them in alive. Their screams could be heard at the camp. It is difficult to say how many children were destroyed in this way.
>
> *Smirnov*: Why did they do this?
>
> *Witness*: It's very difficult to say. We don't know whether they wanted to economize on gas, or if it was because there was not enough room in the gas chambers.[20]

The witness reports correctly what was done. That he errs in his guess as to why it was done is proved by what happened at Ravensbrueck:

> In 1942, the medical services of the Revier were required to perform abortions on all pregnant women. If a child happened to be born alive, it would be smothered or drowned in a bucket, *in the presence of the mother*. Given a new-born child's natural resistance to drowning, a baby's agony might last for twenty or thirty minutes. [Italics added.][21]

Economy did not require the presence of the mothers. The saved gas was no serious factor with the children at Auschwitz. Serious alone was this: 'punishment' of two 'crimes' – Jewish birth, and giving Jewish birth. (Did the Third Reich's thinkers ever settle which 'crime' was worse – and which 'punishment'?)

This conjunction of birth and crime is a *novum* in history. It carries in train a *novum* also in the self-understanding and very being of the two remnants, the Jewish and the Christian. Consider the following:

> There shall be a remnant on Mount Zion and in Jerusalem, as the Lord promised. Anyone who invokes the Lord will be among the survivors. (Joel 3:5.)

Joel refers to Rachel's flesh-and-blood children; Paul (who quotes Joel verbatim [Romans 10:13]), to her spiritual children. Yet the two agree on two commitments, that catastrophe purges, and that the purged remnant – it 'invokes the Lord' – is holy. However, what happened at Auschwitz and Ravensbrueck did not purge. *She'erit ha-pleta*, not a holy but an accidental 'remnant of the destruction' – this is how the survivors have described themselves all along. All along, too, they have referred to those who did not survive as *k'doshim* – 'holy ones'. The very concept of holiness, is the implication, must be altered in response to the conjunction, unprecedented in the annals of history, of 'birth' and 'crime'. The philosophers and theologians, however, have yet to listen.

Auschwitz and Ravensbrueck have changed the very being of the two remnants. As for the flesh-and-blood children of Rachel, they have become children of Job – not the first seven sons and three daughters that died but the second that were given him in their place. As for Rachel's spiritual children, no effort was spared by the planners of Auschwitz and Ravensbrueck to make them into children of Haman.[22]

## 8   The children of Haman

A nightmare vision: a Hitler victory, a Nazi-dominated world. A Jewish remnant? Except for some accidental survivors – a few overlooked here, a few hidden by 'righteous Gentiles' there, all doomed to be the last – , there would be none. A Christian remnant? There are but four possibilities, no more. Then and there, the onward-Christian-soldiers-battle-cry, 'now we are Jews', would have brought the Third Reich down: here and now – the 'here' would be everywhere on earth – it would bring *them* down, those brave Christian-soldiers-come-too-late, dooming them to a Jewish death. Then and there, leaping across the 'Aryan'/'non-Aryan' abyss, a holy Christian remnant survived, thanks to Hitler's defeat: with Hitler victorious, there would be no living Christian heroes, but only dead Christian martyrs. Third, here and now – as of course very prominently then and there – Christians might embrace an 'Aryan' Christ, thus not merely acquiescing in the 'Aryan'/'non-Aryan' dichotomy but giving it their highest endorsement: but, putting it mildly, these would not be Christians. What, then, of a *true* Christian remnant in a Nazi-dominated world? Only one is conceivable: Christian within, 'Aryan' without. In the soul inside, this remnant would reject the un-Christian, anti-Christian, ultimately murderous dichotomy; but in the world outside it would allow itself to be classified 'Aryan'. Without the first, there would be no Christian remnant; without the second, no remnant at all.

A Christian remnant in a Nazi-dominated world: let us view this in Biblical perspective. Like Haman, his modern heir seeks to implicate fellow-Gentiles. Unlike Haman, however, – we picture him victorious world-wide – he seeks to implicate not merely a king, his court, and random groups in one land, but rather all Gentiles – hence all 'non-Aryan' Christians – in all lands. There is, then, a quantitative difference between the old Haman and the new. There is a qualitative one as well. Haman spreads a lie – the Jews 'do not keep the king's laws' (Esther 3:8) – that implicates Gentiles who believe it. The new Haman (who rules Gentiles world-wide, hence Christians world-wide) does more: he implicates all those merely choosing an 'Aryan' life instead of sharing the 'non-Aryan' death. The choice is innocent by all standards one would wish to apply: yet it would leave Christianity in a Nazi-dominated world with but two possibilities: an implicated Christian remnant or no remnant at all.

An implicated Christian remnant: let us view this, too, in Biblical perspective, this time, however, in that of the New Testament of Christians rather than their Old. For Paul catastrophe purges, purges the church, makes it a holy remnant. The Nuremberg laws catastrophe, in contrast, corrupted rather than purged, nay, was meant to corrupt; and – consider the 'Aryan' Christ! – aimed above all, perhaps, at corrupting the Christian churches. Visualise the Nazi Reich victorious world-wide, and the corruption, too, would be world-wide – and inescapable. Then and there, all 'Aryan' survival – hence all 'Aryan'-Christian survival – willy-nilly implied abandoning the 'non-Aryan' Jews to their fate. Here and now, – as we have said, the 'here' would be everywhere on earth – Christian survival would posthumously endorse that abandonment, with a world-now-*judenrein* as a grim and daily reminder. A Christian remnant in a Nazi world, then, would not be purged, could not be holy. It would be, as it were, of Haman's children.

Not all of Rachel's spiritual children were made into Haman's children: the nightmare-vision of Hitler victorious has not come to pass. As this century's greatest man believed in its darkest hour, the mills of God did grind mighty fine. And yet, grind fine though they did, the mills ground slowly – too slowly to prevent the Holocaust. To hark back to Bonhoeffer, may post-Holocaust Christianity, nevertheless, carry on 'seamlessly'? Can its life, its faith, its theological thought be what it was before? Not if the Christian witnesses cited earlier have truth on their side. 'Christians will never get behind Auschwitz, and beyond it . . . only with the victims.'[23]

This sentence sums up the task of the Christian 'Reformation' already referred to. The theologian who wrote it, though German and Catholic, makes it mandatory for post-Holocaust Christianity as a whole. We have seen the 'Reformation' begin with the first two questions of the Bible – the Jewish Ta'nach, the Christian Old Testament. How carry it forward, how assure that it will not go astray?

'Reformation' calls the mind back to the land of the Reformation – also that of the 'Aryan'/'non-Aryan' dichotomy. It also calls the mind back to Martin Luther. The great reformer, we have seen, feared, but also loved, his Old Testament. Esther, in contrast, he hated. 'Oh, how much they [i.e., the Jews] love the Book of Esther which so well fits their bloodthirsty, vengeful, murderous greed and hope.' Note well that Luther's hatred extends here beyond Jews to the Jewish Book, to his own Old Testament. Before and after him, Christians were able to find a message in Esther: why not Luther? Like Augustine, Luther affirms Christian supersessionism. Unlike him a close reader of the Old Testament, he is a close reader of Esther, and thus recognises it as the one Old Testament book that resists Christian supersessionism absolutely, the one book whose 'judaising' – from his point of view as well as in fact – is incorrigible. (For Christians, 'judaising' is any Christian Old Testament reading in its own, rather than New Testament, terms.) Is the 'divine downpour', then, still with the Jews after all? The fear that this might shut him out haunts Luther's Old Testament reading: with Esther it reaches a climax.

Practising apologetics on Luther's behalf, Christians may dismiss his 1542 pamphlet as a scurrilous aberration. With Esther, however, at stake is their own Bible. For Christians, what of Esther, what of Luther's view of the book? Esther's Jews do take vengeance on their Gentile enemies: these had meant to kill them. But do they hate Gentiles as Gentiles? Not with Mordecai serving Ahasverus honestly, not with Esther marrying him. Then who charges Jews with Gentile-hatred? In Esther it is Haman. And Luther? So deep is his fear of 'judaizing' in his own Bible that, on reading Esther, he sides with Haman. For good measure he sides with him also against Jews who on the Purim festival celebrate Haman's downfall – and God's saving power.[24]

On Esther and Jews, Luther wrote what he did in the sixteenth century. The following happened in the twentieth.

> In 1942, during the festival of Purim at Zdunska Wola [a small town in Poland], in revenge of Haman in the time of Ahasverus, 'they' decided to hang ten Polish Jews whose names had been

drawn by lot by the *Judenrat*. Otherwise, the entire Ghetto would be wiped out. When the ten condemned men learned that their deaths would save the Jewish community, they were filled with a strange joy and sang as they stepped to the gallows. The head of the *Judenrat* was forced to give a speech justifying the executioner's work. Twice he fainted; twice he was revived. He had to finish his speech.

But the 'strange joy' of the ten proved premature: their willing death merely postponed the 'wiping out of the entire Ghetto'.

The praxis of 1942 had been prepared by the necessary theory five years earlier. In 1937 I enrolled in my home town university of Halle, being the last Jewish student until, following the *Kristallnacht* of 9 November 1938, I was expelled. There a course was offered entitled 'The Bolshevist Revolution in Russia, the Book of Esther, and the Purim festival of the Jews'. The name of the university of my home town – I was born in it – is *Martin Luther Universitaet*.[25]

After Zdunska Wola of 1942, after *Martin Luther Universitaet* of 1937-8, after Luther himself – what is the touchstone of the required Christian 'Reformation', lest it halt with the first two questions of the Bible, or be carried forward but go astray? Surely Christians must side against Luther's siding with Haman. Surely they must overcome their own fear, age-old though it is, of 'judaising,' for *their required 'destructive recovery' of their own Bible could be described as a re-judaising*. The touchstone? For Jews Esther, a 'strange book' no more, may – perhaps must – be moved from the periphery to the centre of the Jewish Ta'nach: what if the same had to happen to the Christian Old Testament? Perhaps Luther did an unwitting service, in his time, to Christians, in our time. Perhaps his discovery that Esther 's judaising is incorrigible must become a light for post-Holocaust Christianity. Perhaps Esther must become the touchstone, assuring that the Christian 'Reformation' will not go astray. Esther 's Haman is hanged: but his children?

> Then said Esther : 'If it please the king . . . let Haman's ten sons be hanged upon the gallows.' And the king commanded it so to be done . . . and they hanged Haman's ten sons. (Esther 9:13-14.)

Anxious to save Biblical texts, the rabbis explain that his sons must have shared in their father's plot. But after Auschwitz and Ravensbrueck – the children 'punished' for the 'crime' of birth! – this is one text that, though Biblical, cannot be saved. Joel about the remnant – it 'invokes the Lord' and 'survives – has become unsalvageable; so has Esther about Haman's ten sons and the gallows.

*Born Guilty:* this German book[27] recalls the sins of the fathers. Josef Mengele's crimes were such that even reliable reports of the murderous Auschwitz doctor have not ended the world-wide, decades-long search for him.[28] His children, however, are not in hiding but live openly in Germany. The Israeli Mossad has made no attempt to abduct them, nor have survivors tried to punish them in their elusive father's stead. The Mossad and the survivors – these are Jewish witnesses to Germans that birth is innocent, that 'born guilty', even in the case of Haman's children, is unacceptable.

But were Haman's ten sons in fact hanged? A Midrash, bold in the extreme, seems to deny it. No reason exists for the view that Haman had daughters, or that any of his sons had children of their own at the time of their hanging. Yet Haman's children's children, this Midrash asserts, are alive. They teach Torah in B'nai B'rak.[29] B'nai B'rak was famous for Torah-study in Talmudic times. Now a city in Israel, it is famous for Torah-study once more.

## 9    The children of Job

One cannot read Jeremiah's Rachel-text and forget the children, or Job and forget justice. To read the two texts together is to think of justice for the children – the children of Job. His first seven sons and three daughters died when a strong wind caused the roof to collapse upon them while they were feasting in their oldest brother's house. (Job 1:18-19.) Can Job ever forget these, can he reconcile himself to their untimely death, even after the Lord, doubling his former possessions, has given him seven new sons and three new daughters, thus blessing 'his latter end more than his beginning'? (Job 42:10, 12, 13.) Note this well: his former possessions are doubled; but the number of children remains the same. 'While his [i.e., Job's] possessions are doubled, it is a fine trait that the number of children is the same as before.[30] Thus writes the English commentator A. S. Peake, explaining that 'no lost child can be replaced'. Not many have observed this 'fine trait'. Not Rudolf Otto, for whom, the Divine Presence being everything, Job's further recompense is mere 'extra payment thrown in after quittance has already been rendered': Otto gives the children no thought. But then, neither does Hegel, and this even though, unlike Otto's, his Job is not vindicated until 'temporal happiness' is restored to him. But what if no lost child can be replaced? Then vindication remains incomplete even for Hegel's Job, and his 'renunciation of renunciation', a fragment. Abraham dies 'in good old age', 'full of years' (Genesis 25:8), for Isaac lives: how can Job die 'full of days' (Job 42:17), when his first seven sons and three daughters are dead, remain dead – and are irreplaceable?

But *are* children irreplaceable? This can be verified – *made true* – only through a commitment on which those making it stake their lives. (Does Job mourn his lost children to the end of his days? The text is silent.) But lives can also be staked on the opposite commitment – to falsify this belief, *make it false*. Of this the annals of history show no clearer case than the Third Reich. With its Führer alone irreplaceable, it knew, next only to a *judenrein* world, no higher aim – none more passionately pursued – than to make the rest of accessible humanity replaceable. Humans become irreplaceable through personality, and this Hitler's Germany stamped out with stormtroopers' boots. The stormtroopers stamped out their own personalities. In vastly different ways to be sure, they also stamped out those of their victims.

> With the administrative murder of millions death has come to be feared as never before. Every possibility of its somehow becoming part of a person's life as fitting into it is destroyed. The individual is robbed of the last, the poorest that still was his own. In the camps died not the individual but the specimen, and this

fact must affect the dying also of those who escaped the procedure.[31]

These words about death-camp-death are truest about the children. The adults, at least, had become the persons they were in life, prior to being subjected to a specimen-death. But the Auschwitz children? The Ravensbrueck babies? One ponders human nature, human personality, human destiny, and finds no more fearful thought than this: *will these be – are they* already *– as though they never had been*? To push this thought away is impossible; yet so long as a human humanity survives, it is eternally unacceptable.[32] One begins to understand the survivors' meaning when they refer to their dead as *k'doshim* – holy ones.

In beginning to understand, Jews, for their part, also begin to understand themselves as being of the children of Job – the 'Job of the gas chambers'. Of the second sons and daughters who were given to Job in place of the first. As for the first, these are the *k'doshim* who died. But if no lost child can be replaced, how can the *k'doshim*? Then what of the second children of the 'Job of the gas chambers' – post-Holocaust Jewry?

Back in 1951 Martin Buber did not ask about the children of Job, either the first or the second. He did ask, however, two related questions. How is a 'Jewish life' 'still possible after Auschwitz'? For this he substituted, as being 'more correct', how a 'life with God' is still possible 'in a time in which there is an Auschwitz'.[33] To the first two of the three questions the same answer may be ventured: *there must be a possibility, for there is a reality*. The living children cannot – dare not attempt to – replace those who died; yet in writing a new page in Jewish history – *through* founding a new Jewish state but, note this well, not *in* it alone – they can, do, must take their place. Is a 'Jewish life' 'still possible?' This too must be possible, for on that new page it is actual. But – the third question, Buber's 'correct' one – 'in a time in which there is an Auschwitz', can there still be a 'life with God'?

To say that this too must be possible since it is real would be easy – too easy. What if 'reality' were shot through with illusion and irreality? Is this age lacking in cults and fanaticisms, all imagining themselves to be 'lives with God'? Buber's 'correct' question is climactic. Of the three, it is also the most problematic.

Even so I make bold to assert that a Jewish 'life with God' is still possible, for it is real. Where? In Israel, a new Mordecai for a new age in the history of Judaism, guarding the Jewish remnant and obligated to guard it – but strong enough for the task only through hope for help from 'another place'. (Esther 4:14.)

Once, a series of fortunate coincidences helped Mordecai undo Haman. In the most painful possible contrast, coincidences preceding the Holocaust helped the new Haman undo his victims. What if the Great War had never occurred? What if a defeated Germany had not been plagued, first by inflation, then by depression? What if, gassed in the Great War, Hitler had died of it in 1918, or for treason on a hangman's rope in 1923, or by assassination by the brownshirts in 1934, or in a planned army *putsch* in 1938? What if, having lost two million votes in the last free German election, the Führer had been kept out of power in 1933? In 1936, violating the Versailles treaty, he remilitarised the Rhineland: what if the French had marched in? What if in 1938 Chamberlain and Daladier had called the Munich-bluff? To go back from 1938 to 1933, what if civilised countries had retaliated forcefully for 'boycott-of-Jews-day', staged on 1 April of that year? (They did little for Jews in 1933. A decade later, no attempt was made to bomb the Auschwitz railroads.) What if in 1935 the world's Christians, acting on behalf of Jews, but also – note this – on behalf of themselves, had roused themselves with a 'now-we-are-Jews'-battle-cry, bringing down the Nuremberg laws, bringing down the Third Reich? One could heap further coincidence upon coincidence, all happy for the new Haman, all disastrous for his victims: had even one of these 'what ifs' occurred, the Holocaust would not have happened.

A somber but in this context – Israel the new Mordecai – unavoidable thought: with the Holocaust over, the Esthernegating process might have continued. What if British Foreign Secretary Ernest Bevin's post-war anti-Zionist policy had borne fruit? Or the arms embargoes, imposed on 'Palestine' but not on neighbouring Arab states? What if in 1948 David Ben Gurion and his colleagues had accepted, in place of the Jewish state voted for half a year earlier, a 'temporary' United Nations trusteeship? (Chaim Weizmann was right: for a Jewish state, it was either then or not at all.) What if the Jewish state, proclaimed on 14 May 1948, had failed to ward off even one of the armed Arab attacks on its life? Had any of these 'what ifs' occurred, there would today be no 'Jewish life' worthy of the name; the surviving children of Job – broken by Auschwitz but not mended by Jerusalem, would any be left? – would be an accidental remnant, nothing more; and as for a Jewish 'life with God', this would survive only in those circles, orthodox in the extreme, for which, so long as ten male adults survive to recite the daily prayers, nothing ever happens until the Messiah comes.

Thus far at least – the future is unknown – these post-Holocaust anti- Esther 'what-ifs' have not occurred. Why not? Prior to 14 May 1948, because the Yishuv (and a Jewish community supporting it) said 'no' to Bevin, to the embargo, to the United Nations Trusteeship. Ever since that date, because the newly-born state (and, once again, a Jewish community supporting it) has said 'no' to every attempt to destroy it, a new Mordecai protecting the Jewish remnant. However, this new Mordecai is burdened with a grim knowledge beyond the ken of the Biblical: after what has occurred, the time is past for trust in kings or princes; it is past also for trust in fortunate coincidences. Then where is yet 'another place' to look to for help? There must have been such a place these many decades, for without hope for help from it the state could not have guarded the remnant as guard it it must, could not have survived, nay, would never have been proclaimed. A United Nations Trusteeship would have been accepted for 'Palestine'; and by now the trustees would long have presided over the disintegration of the Yishuv. The new page in Jewish history, just barely opened, would have remained blank.

The birth of the state is celebrated on Yom ha-Atzmaut, 'Independence Day'. In synagogues Jews recite Hallel, a thanksgiving liturgy consisting of Psalms 113-18. Fearful of violating the Torah-ordinance against adding to the commandments (Deuteronomy 13:1), some omit the introductory blessings. Others – mourning, perhaps, dead Arabs just as in mid-week Passover Jews mourn drowned Egyptians – recite only 'half-Hallel', omitting parts of Psalms 115 and 116. Others still recite Hallel entire. But whichever the choice, Psalm 118 is being recited, and this begins (and ends) with that very verse that, back in 1951, provoked the question that Buber asked but never answered. He asked it about the 'Job of the gas chambers'. On our part and nearly four decades later, we ask it also about his children. Can either Job or his children – his second ones, for his first ones are dead – give thanks to God, for a Mercy that endureth forever?

For all his pre-Holocaust innocence, Rashi *ad locum*, cautious as ever, projects the problematic thanksgiving into a future beyond history, the Messianic End of Days. Post-Holocaust Jews, however, cannot share Rashi's innocence. Thrust by the Holocaust *into* history, they have had, continue to have, will continue to have, no choice but to *thrust themselves* into history also: this they did, do, must continue to do by restoring, protecting, developing the Jewish state. Of this momentous act many consequences have yet to unfold. One was clear on the first day: 'help' could not wait for the End of Days but was needed for the day after tomorrow. But – the great question shaking the foundations of Judaism in our time – what with 'other places' – Gentile rulers and fortunate coincidences – no longer trustworthy as once they were, what place is left? Ben Gurion, it is said, was filled with foreboding on 14 May 1948, the first Yom ha-Atzmaut; yet he celebrated. Foreboding has been with Jews on every subsequent Yom ha-Atzmaut; yet they too have celebrated and continue to celebrate. How celebrate, how recite Hallel?

Perhaps Buber's unanswered question about a Mercy

enduring forever must remain unanswered still, even four decades later. Perhaps, what with help needed the day after tomorrow, the first verse of Psalm 118 (repeated as last) must be recited *sotto voce* on Yom ha-Atzmaut. But the rest of Hallel, of Psalm 118? What of the celebrating? As times become increasingly troubled for the Jewish state – for the Jewish people – , why do some Jews continue to become Olim – move to the Land of Israel? Why do not more Israeli Jews become Yordim – leave it? Not often asked, these questions come to mind on Yom ha-Atzmaut, and with them the wonder at the fact that the post-Holocaust Esther -negating process was defied and stopped, is being defied and stopped to this day. Why still Olim, why not more Yordim? Because – no other answer is left – some Jews hope, others act as though they hoped, for help coming – some identify it, others not – from 'another place'. A wonder – not unlike that with which Jewish history began in earnest – fills thoughtful Jews on Yom ha-Atzmaut, about that day and all it signifies. Perhaps the more thoughtful they become, the more *sotto voce* also becomes for them one verse of Psalm 118, the one about a Mercy enduring forever. Yet the less *sotto voce* also becomes another, from the same psalm:

> This is the day which the Lord hath made.
> Let us rejoice and be glad in it. (Psalm 118:24.)[34]

## 10   The children of Job and the children of Haman

> O give thanks unto the Lord, for He is good,
> for His mercy endureth forever. (Psalm 118:1, 29.)

The psalmist writing this verse evidently agrees with the author of Psalm 121, who praises a God who keeps Israel, who neither slumbers nor sleeps. Equally evidently, he disagrees with the author of Psalm 44, who seeks to awaken a sleeping God, desperately so because for His sake His people are killed every day. In ascribing all – or nearly all – psalms to the same author – King David – , the rabbis imply the importance of timing. When was it right to compose – is it right to recite – Psalms 121 and 118? When to compose, to recite, Psalm 44?

The question, never far from the minds of Jewish 'generations', has become a life-or-death question for this generation. Hope, murdered at Auschwitz, was resurrected in Jerusalem: can the resurrected hope, ever again, extend to a God never asleep, to a Mercy enduring forever, to an End of Days that will be all praise? In what may be his greatest novel, Elie Wiesel's hero laments that it is too late for the coming of the Messiah, that he – that post-Holocaust Jewry – must manage without him.[35]

The question exists for the flesh-and-blood children of Rachel, made into children of Job. Wishing to share their Book, fraternally, with Rachel's spiritual children, they ask whether the question does not exist for them also – those among them who were made, and those among them who might have been made, into children of Haman. 'We Christians will never again get behind Auschwitz, and beyond it . . . no longer by ourselves, but only with the victims of Auschwitz.' If this is true, how can their Good News be ever-good for Christians unless Jews can give thanks to God for a Mercy enduring forever?

In the Talmud there are various views as to who instituted the custom of Hallel. One answer – unless no psalm was composed prior to David, a sensible one – is Moses and Israel after the Wonder at the Sea, with which Jewish history began in earnest. Sensible too is 'Mordecai and Esther', or it would be so were it not for the fact that the timing is premature, that, as the Talmud has it, they recited Hallel not after Haman was foiled but 'when he rose against them'.

This non-sensible timing gives us pause. That Hallel will be recited – God's Mercy be praised – in a Redemption beyond history the rabbis never doubt. But when within history? On occasions calling for praise, but just on these? The age of prophecy is long past: what if dire times called for faith in self-fulfilling prophecies? For giving thanks to divine Goodness, hoping that this will awaken it? For praising divine Mercy, hoping that this will call it forth? Hallel was ordained, we find in the Talmud, not only for festive celebrations, but also 'for every disaster that threatened but did not occur'.[36]

APPENDIX

## Across the abyss

Text of a Nationally Televised Address delivered in Fulda, Germany on March 6th, 1988, on the Occasion of the Award of the Buber-Rosenzweig Medal to *Studium in Israel*, in Celebration of the Tenth Anniversary of its Existence
*Emil L. Fackenheim* (Translated from the German by the author)

March 6 is a significant day for me. It was the birthday of my older brother, who would be seventy-five years old today if he were still alive. But, the only member of my immediate family unable to escape from Germany in time, he took his life in the Berlin of 1941. Never has the German word *Freitod* had a deeper meaning than in those days. [*Freitod* is a recent alternative for 'suicide' to the previous *Selbstmord* – 'self-murder']. He went freely into death, thus escaping those captors who would have carried him, like other Berlin Jews, off to Treblinka.

I am here today both in spite and because of my brother. That it is in spite of him is obvious to all who are both honest and knowledgeable. These do not talk of *Wiedergutmachung* ['making-things-well-again', the unfortunate German word used for material restitution given to Nazi victims by the Federal Republic – but neither by the German Democratic Republic nor by Austria], or 'overcoming the past', and least of all of the so-called Thousand Year Reich as having been 'so long ago as no longer to be true' [German proverb]. In those twelve years that were for those compelled to suffer them indeed like a thousand, an abyss was torn up that does not have its like in world history and, one hopes, will never have its like. The abyss exists between Germans and Jews, but especially German Jews. Polish and Russian Jews were murdered by enemies. German Jews were murdered by people with whom they had sat, as it were, on the same bench at school, and whose fathers had served in the Great War, shoulder to shoulder, with theirs.

I am therefore here in spite of my brother. If it is also because of him, it is because there must be a possibility of bridging the abyss. If the attempt were not made, Hitler would laugh in hell where he belongs. And his laughter would be the more hellish because the abyss torn up in those days was and is not only between Jews and Germans, but also between Jews and Christians.

Naturally, it was not Christians, or Christians as such, that were guilty of the deed. Yet no thoughtful Christian can doubt that without a tradition that is now widely and rightly described as one of contempt for Jews and Judaism, the Nazi murder of the Jewish people would have been impossible. Just consider this one thing, that while today I am addressing people who are both Germans and Christians, the expression *'Deutsche Christen'* [Nazi-Christians whose main doctrine was that Jesus was an 'Aryan'] is no longer possible, and will never again be possible.

The task is, then, to bridge the abyss that was torn up not only between Jews and Germans but also between Jews and Christians, and above all those who are both Germans and Christians.

As for the abyss between Jews and Christians, I have done throughout my life my share in bridging it. However, when four years ago I moved from Toronto to Jerusalem, I never dreamt that I would get into conversation with young people who are both Christians and Germans, and who are students for a year in Israel. For a Jew today to live in Jerusalem is incomparably meaningful. Yet after four years I can say that for me, now, nothing is more meaningful than conversation with these young people. Without this four-year-experience I would not be here today.

There is a reason: these young Christians from Germany seek to bridge the great abyss from their side. They are in no way responsible for what was done in the time of their grandparents. Yet they voluntarily accept the burden of responsibility, and this because they are hopeful toward the future, and know that this hope is well-grounded only if one takes upon oneself the burden of the past. Germans cannot have Goethe or Hegel and certainly not Heine unless they take upon themselves also Hitler and Heydrich. (From Halle, the place of my birth, comes Haendel but also Heydrich, one of the worst.) And Christians cannot have Augustine, the saint, and Luther, the herald of freedom, without taking upon themselves the burden of the fact that Augustine fell prey to the slander that Jews are children not of Abraham but of Cain; and that Luther was the malignant hater of Jews who demanded, centuries prior to *Kristallnacht*, that the synagogues should be set on fire.

How can young people who are both Germans and Christians attempt to bridge this two-fold abyss? In no better way than that trodden by those with whom I have been in conversation for four years.

These days one hears quite a few declarations by Christian organisations, to the effect that antisemitism is un-Christian, or even that despite the 'new' Israel the 'old' still has a certain validity. However, in view of so long a tradition of Christian teaching of contempt for Jews and Judaism, Jews have reason to remain sceptical about these declarations, and unfortunately this skepticism is often borne out by experience. Thus, for example, there was the Vatican II Conference – and then an audience for Kurt Waldheim by the Vatican. Or again, rightist antisemitism is condemned by a church – and then reappears, disguised as anti-Zionism, on the left. What can be done by Christians to make, at long last, a real end to the miserable tradition of Jew-hatred in the religion of love?

Nothing better, I believe, than what these young people are doing, namely, to study Jewish texts. Through the centuries Christians have imagined that Jews spend their days rejecting the Christ, or to put it into worse words, killing him all over again, just as they are said to have done originally. If a Christian studies the post-Biblical texts of Judaism seriously and honestly, he discovers with astonishment that, except in relation to Christians, the Christ of Christianity does not occur at all in the teachings of Judaism. Has it ever happened before that, except for purposes of slandering it, Christians have studied the Talmud seriously? Rarely. Why was it necessary to slander the Talmud? Have Christians, including worthy professors, been so insecure in their Christian faith that such slander was needed? If so, there was not much to their faith.

The young people, who have been sent, already for ten years, by the study-circle *Studium in Israel* evidently do not suffer from such fears, for they come in order to study the Talmud seriously and honestly. And what do they discover? For example, the declaration that God created only one human pair, in order that nobody might be able to say that his remote ancestor was better than that of another! Can there be a more magnificent example of anti-racist thinking? Or the passage that adjures heaven and earth that all are equal, whether man or woman, Jew or Gentile, that all depends on this, whether a person directs his heart to heaven? Does this not sound like the apostle Paul, despite the fact that a Jew does not go the way through the Christ? Should a Christian not rejoice in the fact that his older brother discovered this on his own, and that he testifies, moreover, that Gentiles too can discover it? Might this discovery not help liberate Christians from the narrow Constantinian doctrine (which makes life so hard for them today) that there is no redemption outside the church?

If it is a hope-inspiring fact that these young people, as Christians, study Jewish texts, it is hope-inspiring as well that, as Germans, they pursue this study in Jerusalem. On this crucial point, there is for them simply no choice. For if, after what has occurred, there is still Jewish faith at all, it is, I am convinced, exclusively because of the fact that after the great catastrophe there arose a Jewish state. Through the centuries the Jewish people never forgot Jerusalem. After the Holocaust this people would have fallen prey to despair, had they not returned to Jerusalem. Never was Jewish statelessness so great a catastrophe as during the rule of the Third Reich. And in no time could the rebirth of a Jewish state be a blessing as great as today. There are people today in many countries, Germany included, that no longer wish to see this, and certainly Israel has many unsolved problems, such as that of the Palestinian Arabs. But these must not be allowed to obscure the insight – as expressed, for example, by the German Catholic theologian Johann Baptist Metz – that Israel is a 'house against death'. There are many Arab countries, and they are houses for life. Israel is the only house of the Jewish people, and it still is a house against death. Were it destroyed, Hitler would have his last victory. In that case there would be, after four millennia, an end to the Jewish people. However, here too hope must have the last word – the hope that one day Israel too will be a house, not against death, but for life. But people endowed with insight understand that this is not yet the case, and probably will not be the case in our time.

The study-circle *Studium in Israel* knows all this. The young people who belong to the study-circle are learning it, led by their most understanding guide, Dr. Michael Krupp. They are engaged in building the two-fold bridge to the Jewish people – as Christians, and as Germans. They are witnesses to hope. Hence it is a matter of greatest satisfaction for me, a Jewish refugee from Germany, to return to Germany, in order to pay tribute to a study circle whose work creates hope for a Jewish, a Christian, a German future.

Once Hegel, the greatest German philosopher, observed that the wounds of the spirit heal without leaving scars. This he could no longer say today. Scars do remain, and 'healing' is not the right word. But to alleviate the pain is possible, and this is why we are here today.

### Response

*Astrid Fiehland, Pastorin* in Kiel (Translated from the German by E. L. F.)

With great joy I accept the honour bestowed by the *Deutsche Koordinierungsrat [der Gesellschaften fuer Christlich-Juedische Zusammenarbeit E. V.]* on the study-circle *Studium in Israel* for its decade of work.

Representing all those who since 1978 have spent a year of study at Hebrew University, I would like today to thank those who paved our way to Jerusalem: first, the Jewish partners in Germany and Israel who – despite the Holocaust – were willing to work together with Germans and Christians. But I would also like to thank those Christians and theologians who, after 1945, were not satisfied with a quickly-formulated confession of guilt, but worked for a genuine *Umkehr* [Turning, *T'shuva*, *Metanoia*] of Christians in relation to the Jewish people. Our generation is able to carry on where they left off, and feels under an obligation to their work.

To be allowed to live and study for a year in Jerusalem has been a formative experience for us all. What we learned there in our encounter with Judaism determines our theological thinking still, but also the way in which we read the Hebrew Bible and the New Testament. The study of the language, and above all the discovery of the world of rabbinic interpretation of Scripture in Midrash and Talmud – a world largely unknown to us Christians – has made us understand much anew of what has become alien to us in our own tradition, or even forgotten long ago.

To live in the Land, however, also is to become sensitive to those unresolved conflicts, the disquieting consequences of which are before our eyes in just the present weeks.

Finally, as Germans we come in Israel upon traces of our own history. One of the most moving experiences of my own year of study was a meeting with a group of young Israelis, whose parents survived the annihilation camps of the Nazis. After some hesitation this group of young people – children of the second and third generation like ourselves – invited us to one of their meetings. For quite a few this was the first time they had talked with Germans. What they told us that evening is engraved deep in my memory. I became aware of what wounds are left, even in the lives of the children, by the nameless anxiety and the horrifying agonies that their parents had to suffer in the Nazi death camps. On their behalf as well as our own, I am filled with shame and anger by the fact that today the demand is being made, increasingly self-confidently, that at long last a *Schlussstrich* [final line] should be drawn to the German past.

I cannot let go of a question we were asked that evening: what does it mean to you, to be the children of those who did it? We are asked that question as Germans but must answer it also as Christians. What is our attitude toward a Christian theology that is not only implicated in the centuries-old history of contempt for Jews but has even produced it itself?

There are today encouraging beginnings of a changed Christian theology, that is no longer guided by the traditional, polemical self-demarcation from Judaism, but emphasises the shared task of Jews and Christians in the world. However, we must not deceive ourselves about the fact that in wider circles little has as yet changed in the Christian attitude toward Jews.

The intensive study of Jewish sources has sharpened our insight into how shallow and often enough negative our textbooks and even more recent theological literature, are among us on 'Jews', or 'Pharisees'. And ignorance has always fed prejudices!

It is a serious and necessary step to listen to how Jews themselves understand their faith and their religious traditions.

To this end there is no better way than to live in Israel, to study Torah with Jews, to celebrate their festivals with them, and to pray with them in their synagogues. In the end one will recognise: a year is not enough for the understanding of Judaism in its many facets. Many of us go back, to deepen what has been learned – and also to see friends again.

But our work is here in Germany. What we have learned, we take with us into our congregations, our schools, our churches. Many of us are engaged today in Jewish–Christian dialogue, in the labour of reconciliation, and with other groups whose aim is to secure the traces of history and to offer determined resistance to all new signs of racist thinking.

A beginning has been made. Putting it to the proof is a task that still lies still ahead.

# NOTES

## Foreword

1 An allusion to the *Lecha Dodi*, a much-beloved Shabbat hymn, in which the Shabbat is described as 'first in thought but last in work'.

2 See 'New hearts and the old covenant', *The Divine Helmsman*, J. L. Crenshaw & S. Sandmel, eds. (New York: Ktav, 1980), 191 ff.; reprinted in *The Jewish Thought of Emil Fackenheim*, M. Morgan, ed. (Detroit: Wayne State University Press 1987), 223 ff.

3 On this subject see more fully my *To Mend the World: Foundations of Post-Holocaust Jewish Thought*, second ed. (New York: Schocken, 1989, subsequently cited as *To Mend*), ch. IV, sec. 11, 'Historicity, hermeneutics and Tikkun Olan after the Holocaust'.

4 How this book fits into my original plan may be learned from *To Mend*, ch.I, sec.5. A reading of *To Mend* as a whole will show how it emerges from my thought as a whole.

5 See below, ch.4, sec. 1.

## Chapter I

1 Midrash is the profoundest theology ever developed in Judaism, the more so because it is not 'theology' – the logos of God offered, as it were, from the standpoint of God – but parables, stories and the like, given from the standpoint of man and hence often mutually contradictory. This view of Midrash informs all my previous books. For a Midrashic treatment of the 'binding' of Isaac ('binding' to stress that the sacrifice did not take place), see my *Encounters Between Judaism and Modern Philosophy* (New York: Schocken, 1980), 53 ff. (henceforth cited as *Encounters*).

2 On Hegel, see my *The Religious Dimension in Hegel's Thought* (University of Chicago Press, 1982, henceforth cited as *RD*). On Hegel on Judaism, see *Encounters*, ch. 3 and *To Mend*, ch. 3. See also below, ch. 4, sec. 3.

3 In medieval thought the belief in Revelation is typically based on sacred authority. Beginning with Kierkegaard, religious existentialism is best understood as putting an admittedly subjective 'commitment' into the place left vacant by the modern–critical destruction of intellectual authorities, sacred ones included. See further *To Mend*, ch.2 and my *What is Judaism?* (New York: Collier, 1988), chs. 1 and 4 (henceforth cited as *WiJ*).

4 Ta'nach – an abbreviation of 'Torah', *'N'vi'im'* ('Prophets'), *'K'tuvim'* ('Writings') is the proper designation of the Jewish Bible within Judaism. That I have no objection to 'Old Testament' within Christianity will

Notes

appear in context, although Christian readers may wish to substitute, in thought if not words, 'old-new' – oddly reminiscent of Theodor Herzl's 'Old-Newland' for Palestine-Eretz Israel.

5 This is the main burden of *RD*.

6 In his Introduction to Ludwig Feuerbach, *The Essence of Christianity* (New York: Harper Torchbooks, 1957), xix.

7 On Feuerbach and his followers, see *Encounters*, 134-52. See also Ernst Bloch, *Das Prinzip Hoffnung* (Frankfurt: Suhrkamp, 1959), e.g.1412 ff.,1456 ff.,1464 ff.

8 'Atheistische Theologie,' *Kleinere Schriften* (Berlin: Schocken, 1937), 285 (henceforth cited as *AT*).

9 An allusion to the subtitle of D. F. Schleiermacher's *Reden über die Religion*, delivered in Berlin in 1799. The *Reden* had an enormous impact at the time.

10 *Franz Rosenzweig: his Life and Thought*, N. N.Glatzer, ed. (New York: Schocken, 1967), 28. These words adorned a poster prominently displayed during an International Rosenzweig Congress held in his native city of Kassel in 1986. The Proceedings were published as *Der Philosoph Franz Rosenzweig*, two vols., W. Schmied-Kowarzik, ed. (Munich: Alber, 1988).

11 Preface (to the English edition of Leo Strauss, *Spinoza's Critique of Religion, The Jewish Expression*, J. Goldin, ed. (New York: Bantam, 1970), 352 ff. See also, for the whole present subject, *WiJ*, ch. 1, in which I already cite Strauss's statement.

12 On the Spinoza-Rosenzweig relation, see *To Mend*, ch.2, which also contains my present understanding of the *Star*.

13 London: Oxford, 1935, 234.

14 *Lessing's Theological Writings*, H. Chadwick, tr. & ed. (London: Adam & Charles Black, 1956), 51 ff.

15 'The Man of Today and the Jewish Bible', *Israel and The World* (New York: Schocken, 1963), 89, 94, 96 ff.

16 J.D.Levenson, *Sinai and Zion* (Minneapolis: Winston, 1985), 15.

17 Franz Rosenzweig, *Briefe* (Berlin: Schocken, 1935), 582.

18 *The Prophetic Faith* (New York: Macmillan, 1949), 179. This passage should be read together with Buber's searching critique of Carl Jung in *Eclipse of God* (New York: Harper Torchbooks, 1952), 78 ff.,133 ff.

19 An authoritative example is Brevard S. Childs's *Introduction to the Old Testament as Scripture* (Philadelphia: Fortress Press, 1979). Childs cites Buber only three times. Yet his work is monumental in that it treats the Jewish Bible 'as Scripture' as well as an object of scholarship, and as the Jewish Ta'nach as well as the Christian Old Testament.

20 'The Man of Today and the Jewish Bible', op.cit., 93, 89.

21 A good example is Karl Jaspers, *Die Geistige Situation der Zeit* (Berlin: de Gruyter, 1931). As students in Berlin after 1933, we all took this (probably correctly) as a critique of Nazism but also of modernity as a whole. I cite Jaspers rather than Heidegger because the latter's arrogant

notion of Germany as the 'metaphysical *Volk*' is alien to him. On Heidegger, see *To Mend*, part IV.

22 The preceding is much indebted to Eberhard Bethge's magisterial *Dietrich Bonhoeffer* (New York: Harper & Row, 1970).

23 My letters to Bethge are published in part in *The Jewish Thought of Emil Fackenheim*, M. Morgan, ed. (Detroit: Wayne State University Press, 1987), 241-3. For Bethge's two addresses, see *Konsequenzen: Dietrich Bonhoeffer's Kirchenverstaendnis Heute*, E. Feil & I. Toedt, eds. (Munich: Chr. Kaiser, 1980), 171-214, especially 173, 202, 209 ff. and *Ethik im Erstfall: Dietrich Bonhoeffer's Stellung zu den Juden und ihre Aktualitaet*, W. Huber & I. Toedt, eds. (Munich: Chr. Kaiser, 1982), 30-40. Bethge's first essay ends as follows:

> Bonhoeffer is not the orginator of such a [i.e., post-Holocaust Christian] theology. But he belongs to those who made it possible . . . He was one of the few who had liberated himself of complicity with the practitioners of the 'Final Solution'. This makes him into an indispensable bond with the victims, the survivors and the descendants of the Holocaust. Evidently, the theme which on our side is 'Bonhoeffer and the Jews' must have a dialogical counterpart from the other side in 'The Jews and Bonhoeffer'. (Op.cit., 212.)

Bethge's *Dietrich Bonhoeffer und die Juden* has appeared in English in *Ethical Responsibility: Dietrich Bonhoeffer's Legacy to the Churches* (Lewiston, NY: Edwin Mellen Press, 1981), 43 ff. I am immeasurably indebted to Bethge, his private letters to me as well as his publications.

24 The essay is conveniently found in *Essays on Old Testament Hermeneutics*, C.Westermann,ed. (Atlanta: John Knox Press, 1963), 50-75. 'Seamless' remains also the theology of most of the other contributors to the *Essays*, with one *novum* – a Jewish state – here and there recognised but not the other, the Holocaust. As though this latter were, perhaps, a Jewish but in no sense a Christian catastrophe, W. Zimmerli writes: 'The new aspect of awaiting fulfilment is that fulilment can bring nothing more than the open unveiling of that which is already fulfilled.' (Op.cit., 114.)

25 The radio talk is conveniently available in *Against the Stream* (London: SCM Press, 1954), 193-202.

26 *Church Dogmatics* II 2 (Edinburgh: T. &. T. Clark, 1957), 195 ff. and *passim*. The cited passages are found on 214, 201, 198, but for a full impact the whole text should be read.

27 Op. cit., 201.

28 See below, ch. 4.

29 See Bethge in *Konsequenzen*, 198, 200.

30 See *Ethik im Ernstfall*, 29. According to the editors Peck's 'Answer' was a 'vote' given immediately after the first Bethge address. This Bethge had begun by stating that there was no hope for a Christian post-Holocaust theology unless it was preceded by an *Erschuetterung* (being-shaken-to-

the core) of the Christian soul by the event itself. Evidently Peck was one Christian *erschuettert* by what he had heard.

**31** *I and Thou*, W. Kaufmann, tr. (New York: Scribners, 1970), 157.

**32** *Eclipse of God*, 23. In a memorable meeting my wife and I had with Buber during his 1958 Princeton visit, he responded to my view that since *I and Thou* he had changed his mind as to whether God speaks constantly, by strongly hinting that not his mind but reality had changed.

**33** *At the Turning; Three Addresses on Judaism* (New York: Farrar, Straus & Young, 1952), 61. Buber's question will inform the whole rest of this book, with full attention to it only at the end. Buber himself, having stressed the divine-human estrangement after Auschwitz, ends *At the Turning* as follows: 'We do not put up with earthly being, we struggle for its redemption, and struggling we appeal to the help of our Lord, Who again and still is a hiding one . . . Though His coming appearance resemble no earlier one, we shall recognize again our cruel and merciful Lord.' (Op. cit., 62.) I have commented on this end in *To Mend*, 197. My preface to the second edition of that work is my most comprehensive statement of why I find Buber's 'eclipse of God' insufficient in response to the Holocaust. Still less adequate to me is a divine 'cruelty' – if connected with the Holocaust. On both aspects see also the last chapter of *WiJ*.

## Chapter II

**1** Martin Buber, *Moses* (New York: Harper Torchbooks, 1958), 75. My *God's Presence in History* (New York: Harper Torchbooks, 1970, 12-13, henceforth cited as *Presence*) begins in earnest, so to speak, with the 'Song at the Sea' itself, as well as a lengthy citation from *Moses* on the 'permissible' concept of miracle. The reader may wish to ponder why, in contrast, the present account of a 'history that almost was not,' begins in earnest with the event at Marah.

**2** Whereas Moses is identied by Maimonides as the 'chief of the prophets' traditionally he is referred to as *Moshe Rabbenu*.

**3** 'Salvation History'. The meaning of this term will more fully appear in context, becoming thematic in its contrast to flesh-and-blood history in ch.3.

**4** See *Iture Torah*, Aharon Y. Greenberg, ed. (Tel Aviv: Yavneh, 1965), III, 129.

**5** *The Interpreter's Bible*, G. A. Buttrick, ed. (Nashville: Abingdon, 1952), I, 948.

**6** We thus begin here the first of our three applications, to the 'naked text' of the Jewish Bible, of the post-Holocaust hermeneutic, first defined in its own context in *To Mend*, IV, ch. 11, and developed for the present context in the first chapter of this book.

**7** See Buber, *Moses*, 105.

**8** See Rosenzweig, *AT*, 290. The essay was written in the spring of 1914, in response to Buber's invitation, for inclusion in a volume on Judaism, but rejected as unsuitable, and the volume itself never appeared. The German 'Wissenschaft,' unlike the English 'science,' includes scholarship insofar as it claims an objectivity no less great than the natural sciences. See further ch.4 section 5. On left-wing Hegelians and Judaism, see further *Presence*, ch.2, *Encounters*, ch.3, *To Mend*, part III, ch. 9. The appalling exploitability of these nineteenth-century thinkers has been revealed, and continues to be revealed, only in the appalling twentieth century. Wiser than the left-wing Hegelians because religiously-motivated even in his most extreme anti-religious fulminations, Nietzsche seems to have feared this possibility, see below n. 11.

**9** At the time of writing, the Palestinian Liberation Organisation has given no indication of willingness to revoke its 1964 'Covenant' – the most appalling ideological-political document since *Mein Kampf* – which calls for the violent destruction of the State of Israel along with the expulsion (if not worse) of most of its Jewish inhabitants. Nor has the United Nations Organisation shown signs of revoking its Zionism-is-Racism resolution, the most influential (as well as inflammatory) antisemitic statement since the Holocaust. In these circumstances it is astounding that more Jews do not leave Israel; that some continue to come; that the 'leftist' Peace Now movement moves heaven and earth for the sake of peace with the Arab neighbours, even as the 'rightist'-religious Gush Emunim clings to a God who will move this 'piece of earth' (Buber, see ch.3, sec. 1) so as fully to restore the Jewish bond with it, and create peace. All this is the more remarkable since Israel is the only country in the world that mourns individually each and every one of its fallen soldiers.

**10** See above, ch. 1, n. 16.

**11** 'Over-humanity' is an allusion to Nietzsche, 'pagan', to Rosenzweig. For this latter on the divine bridging, see *AT*, 290. On relevant passages in Nietzsche's *Zarathustra*, see *Werke* (Leipzig: Kroener, 1919), vol. 5, e.g. 27, 43 ff., 84 ff., 163 ff., 268, 293 ff., 306, 467 ff. My remarks on Nietzsche's fears of the possible effects of his work are based on passages such as the following:

> You express your will for the free heights, your soul thirsts for the stars. However, your evil drives also thirst for freedom. (61) The earth is full of superfluous ones (63) – yet for these the state was invented. (70) Invisibly the world turns on the inventors of new values, yet the people and glory turns on the actors. The actor may have spirit, but little spiritual conscience. He always believes what he can make others believe, make others believe in him. (73 ff.)

(On Hitler as actor, see my 'Holocaust and *Weltanschauung*: philosophical reflections on why they did it,' *Holocaust and Genocide Studies*, III, 2, 1988, 197 ff.)

> You lonely ones of today . . . , from you, the self-chosen, one day shall grow a chosen *Volk* – and from this the Overman (114)

Most frightened-frightening is the following:

> When I looked into the mirror I screamed and my heart was *erschuettert*: for I saw not myself in the mirror but the grimace and jeering laughter of a devil. (120) [The translations are mine. After the quotation from Bethge in ch.1, I leave *Erschuetterung* untranslated.]

Well aware of the fact that the edition from which I quote will be unavailable to most, I do use this edition for two reasons. (1) The reader should read *Zarathustra* entire – with *Exodus* next to him. (2) *Werke* as cited by me was published when World War I was hardly over, and contains the texts in the (uncritical) form read by hundreds of thousands. I inherited the edition from my mother, who was given it by my father in 1920, and who certainly read it with the war just ended in mind. By the time I was old enough to exchange views with her she was no longer alive. Did Hitler read *Zarathustra*? References to the Overman and 'man as the becoming God' are comparably rare. Yet R. G. L. Waite rightly stresses the fact that *Zarathustra* had a *Kriegsausgabe* which, it is said, the German military authorities offered their soldiers for their knapsack, as a gift alternative to the Bible. That Corporal Hitler should have chosen the Bible is unthinkable. On 'Nietzsche and Hitler', see Waite, *The Psychopathic God: Adolf Hitler* (New York: Basic Books, 1977), 275 ff.

12 On Yom Kippur see Franz Rosenzweig, *The Star of Redemption* (Holt, Rinehart & Winston 1971), 323 ff., 367. On Rosenzweig on Yom Kippur, see *To Mend*, part II, chs. 3-5, and my 'The systematic role of the Matrix (Existence) and the Apex (Yom Kippur) of Jewish religious life in Rosenzweig's *Star of Redemption*', *Der Philosoph Franz Rosenzweig*, W. Schmied-Kowarzik, ed. (Freiburg: Alber, 1988), vol. II, 567 ff.

13 The Hanuka-hymn may be found in any edition of the traditional prayerbook, the *Siddur*; the *Dayyenu*, in any traditional edition of the Passover-*Haggadah*.

14 See Chaim Kaplan, *Scroll of Agony*, tr. and ed. A. I. Katsh (New York: Macmillan, 1965), 213 ff., 321 ff., 340; *The Warsaw Diary of Adam Czerniakow*, R. Hilberg, S. Staron, J. Kermisz, eds. (New York: Stein & Day, 1979), 384, 70. From the many sources available I cite Kaplan and Czerniakow, for two different – perhaps even opposed – perspectives within the Warsaw Ghetto. For a Nazi account from without it, Claude Lanzmann's masterful film *Shoah* should be seen entire. The Nazi commissioner of the Warsaw Ghetto was Dr Heinz Auerswald. Astonishingly, Lanzmann was able to interview Auerwald's deputy, Dr Franz Grassler, a man mentioned numerous times in Czerniakow's *Diary*. Grassler began by remarking that he remembered his pre-war mountaineering better than his Warsaw Ghetto activities since, 'thank God,' one 'tends to forget . . . the bad times more easily than the good'. Offered

Lanzmann's help to remember, Grassler went on to say that he had wished to see of the Ghetto as little as possible; that he was worried about an outbreak of typhus since it might have spread to 'the Poles and the Germans'; that he 'knew nothing' of extermination, 'of course'; that if ever he knew how many died of starvation, he did not know now; that Czerniakow committed suicide because he 'realised there was no future for the Ghetto' – this because he was 'much better informed' than such as Grassler himself, for he was only a nonentity.

The interview which begins with Grassler's mountain-climbing ends as follows:

> *Lanzmann*: You had a doctorate.
> *Grassler*: The title proves nothing.
> *Lanzmann*: Doctor of Law . . . What did you do after the war?
> *Grassler*: I was with a mountaineering house. I wrote and published mountain guide books. I published a mountain climbers' magazine.
> *Lanzmann*: Is climbing your main interest?
> *Grassler*: Yes.
> *Lanzmann*: The mountains, the air . . .
> *Grassler*: Yes.
> *Lanzmann*: The sun, the pure air . . .
> *Grassler*: Not like Ghetto air.

(Claude Lanzmann, *Shoah: an Oral History of the Holocaust, the Complete Text of the Film* (New York: Pantheon, n.d.), 175-194.) Simone de Beauvoir begins her preface to the book version as follows: '*Shoah* is not an easy film to talk about . . . After the war we [meaning, I think, Jean-Paul Sartre and herself] read masses of accounts of the ghettos and extermination camps, and we were devastated. But when, today, we see Claude Lanzmann's extraordinary film, we realize we have understood nothing . . . (vii). Beauvoir died soon after she wrote these words, and Sartre had died before her. To my knowledge no philosopher has yet responded to *Shoah*, at least trying to understand.

## Chapter III

1 Gandhi published his piece in his paper *Harijan* (*The untouchable*) on 28 November 1938, i.e. less than two weeks after the so-called *Kristallnacht* in which synagogues in Nazi Germany had been burned, Jewish stores smashed and looted, and Jewish men above sixteen had disappeared one did not dare to enquire where. Had I, myself imprisoned in Sachsenhausen, followed Gandhi's advice and practised *Satyagraha* – nonviolent resistance to the stormtroopers – , I would not have savoured the moral victory he said would follow, for they would have shot me on the spot. Nor would anyone else have savoured my victory, for my family would have been sent my ashes, together with a bill for postage and an explanation, perhaps, that I had died of typhus or been

shot while trying to escape.

On Zionism – in this context the relevant subject – , Gandhi forgot that he himself had made two demands on behalf of Indians, one, a liberated state, the other, equality in South Africa. He must have forgotten, for he rejected Jewish nationalism, on the grounds that Jews could not claim both civil rights elsewhere and a country of their own. He even suggested that, in being Zionist, Jews gave 'colorable justification' to antisemitic charges of dual loyalty.

In April 1939, the Jerusalem group 'The Bond' published a pamphlet by that name (Jerusalem: Rubin Mass), reprinting Gandhi's article and responses by J.L.Magnes and Buber. As Maurice Friedman points out, whereas Magnes addressed the Indian leader as 'Dear Mr Gandhi', Buber showed his reverence by addressing him as 'Mahatma'. Reverence, too, would seem to be the reason for his letter's quality – perhaps Buber's best statement of his Zionism. Excerpts of Gandhi's and Buber's texts are readily available in Buber anthologies.

Maurice Friedman's massive three-volume *Martin Buber's Life and Work* (New York: Dutton, 1983) – indispensable for in-depth Buber-study – has a good account of the Gandhi-Buber episode: vol. 2, 172 ff., 288 ff.

2 A good example is Isaac Deutscher, *The Non-Jewish Jew* (London: Oxford, 1968). Ever since the Emancipation Jews have been apt to wish to merge with mankind-in-general. However, what with Stalin's betrayal of the international proletariat in the communist East, persisting nationalism in the liberal West and, of course, Hitler, this process has increasingly become a Jewish wish-to-merge-with-'mankind' – without mankind. Deutscher makes a virtue of this tragic – or is it tragicomic? – condition by projecting 'mankind' into the future, and by considering the vanguard of this future mankind to consist of 'non-Jewish Jews' such as Marx, Trotsky and himself.

3 Unbelievably, this was done by a group of the ultra-orthodox N'ture Karta. In present Iran, they were perhaps the only Jews welcome.

4 Yehuda Amital, *Ha-ma'alot Mi-ma'amakim* (Jerusalem: Alon Sh'vut, 1973).

5 On this whole subject see my *To Mend*, part IV, chs. 14, 15 and part V; *WiJ*, part III; and *A Political Philosophy for the State of Israel: Fragments* (Jerusalem Centre for Public Affairs, 1988), 18 pp.

6 Commenting on Genesis 15:13-18 (the divine promise of the Land to Abraham and his seed), E. A. Speiser writes: 'The documentary source of this passage is still unclear. There can be no doubt, however, about the significance of the contents in Israelite historical thought. The covenant between God and Israel was the charter on which Israel's national position was founded.' (*Genesis* (New York: Doubleday, 1964), 113.) 'Turning point' is the term used by Nehama Leibowitz with reference to Exodus 2:22-5 (*Studies in Shemot*, part I (World Zionist Organisation, 1976), 18).

**7** This expression sticks in my mind from H. H. Guthrie Jr., *Israel's Sacred Songs* (New York: Seabury Press, 1966), 160 where he also speaks of the 'offensiveness of many lines in Israel's songs'. On p. 131 he writes: 'It is precisely a deep conviction of Yahweh's righteous, dependable rule that is the source of Israel's blatant querying of Him in the face of meaningless disaster . . . '. The observation seems fair enough: but why is the querying 'blatant'? It should be added, however, that both Calvin and Luther found precisely the stormy heart of the Psalmist meaningful for the Christian reader.

**8** This text may be found in the Rosh ha-Shanah Mussaf prayer in any traditional High Holy Day prayer book.

**9** See also my comment on this same *Ezekiel* chapter in *WiJ*, 125 ff.

**10** See further below, ch. 4, sec. 4.

**11** B. S. Childs, *Introduction to the Old Testament as Scripture* (Philadelphia: Fortress Press, 1979), 644.

**12** Canon and canonicity are, as it were, sub-themes in this book. When Buber wrote of 'Biblia' as 'one book' (above, ch. 1, sec.2), he invoked a unifying principle other than its canonicity. What is now coming under questioning, however cursorily, is directly that principle, and indirectly the canonicity of the Jewish Bible. A thorough investigation of this latter theme is desirable, and would be greatly assisted by S. Z. Leiman, *The Canonization of Hebrew Scripture: the Talmudic and Midrashic Evidence* (Hamdon: Archon Books, 1976).

**13** Schalom Ben Chorin's *Kritik Des Estherbuches* (Jerusalem: Heatid, 1938) appeared prior to the Holocaust, his *Als Gott Schwieg* (Mainz: Gruenewald, 1986), forty years after. In my view, this is the total and wholly adequate cause for the sharp contrast between a 1938 fideism so close to a Christian as to demand the elimination of Esther from the canon, and *Als Gott Schwieg* in which surviving Jews have much to say – 'after God was silent'.

On Esther and Christians in general, Luther in particular, see further ch. 4, sec. 8.

Elias Bickerman, *Four Strange Books in the Bible* (New York: Schocken, 1984) deals with Jonah, Daniel, Koheleth and Esther. Of these, surely Esther is strangest.

**14** On Haman and Hitler, see further below, ch.4 sec.8, as well as the Preface to the second edition of *To Mend*.

**15** See below, ch. 4, sec. 9.

**16** See further below, ch. 4, sec. 8.

**17** See n. 12.

**18** See *RD*, 136 ff.

**19** When Rome ordered a Caligula statue for the Jerusalem Temple, the Jewish–Roman war threatened by this act was averted only by Caligula's assassination, in 41 CE.

**20** In my view the crucial argument against Aristotle in the *Guide for the Perplexed* is for creation, and against the eternity of the universe.

## Notes

21 Arthur Koestler, *Promise and Fulfilment* (London: Macmillan & Co., 1949), 335. To show that Koestler was indeed a man of his time one need go no further than list three brilliant novels: *Darkness at Noon* – on communism; *Thieves in the Night* – on the more militant segments of Zionism; *Arrival and Departure* – one of the earliest novels on the Holocaust.

22 'The Malbim' is the nineteenth century scholar Meir Loeb ben Yechiel Michael. His interpretation, based on Bab. Talmud Baba Bathra 15 ff., is given no stronger encouragement by the Talmudic text than its failure to cite Job 1:19, the passage in which the death of the children is reported.

23 See P. Schindler, *Responses of Hasidic Leaders and Hasidim During the Holocaust in Europe, 1939-45* (Ann Arbor: University Microfilms, 1972), 102 ff.

24 See Halina Birenbaum, *Hope is the Last to Die* (New York: Twayne, 1971).

## Chapter IV

1 In *Church Dogmatics* II 2 (Edinburgh: T. & T. Clark, 1957), 201.

2 Thus F. W. Marquardt, who has also informed me that what, other than failing health, caused Barth to suspend work on the *Church Dogmatics* after his return from America remains yet to be explored.

3 'Religious values after the Holocaust: a Catholic view', *Jews and Christians after the Holocaust*, A. J. Peck, ed. (Philadelphia: Fortress Press, 1982), 87 ff. See also his foreword to A. A. Cohen, *The Tremendum* (New York: Crossroad, 1981).

4 Both at a meeting in London in June 1988, in conclusion of the largest Holocaust scholars' conference ever, held in Oxford.

5 Thus the Jewish historian Heinrich Graetz.

6 That no less heroic an anti-Nazi Christian than Martin Niemoeller was himself infected with antisemitism is shown by Robert Michael, 'Theological myth, German antisemitism and the Holocaust: the case of Martin Niemoeller', *Holocaust and Genocide*, II, 1, 1987, 105 ff.

7 Quoted in Martin Stoehr, 'Martin Luther und die Juden', *Christen und Juden*, W. Marsch & K. Thieme, eds. (Mainz: Matthias Gruenewald Verlag, 1961), 140.

8 Dietrich Eckart, *Der Bolschevismus von Moses bis Lenin: Zwiegespraech Zwischen Adolf Hitler und Mir* (Munich: Eher Verlag, 1924).

9 On the above see G. W. F. Hegel, 'On the Positivity of the Christian religion', *Early Theological Writings*, T.M. Knox & R. Kroner, eds. (University of Chicago Press, 1948), especially 149.

10 See *RD*, passim.

11 On this subject see *Encounters*, 79-169.

12 For Hegel on Job, see *Vorlesungen Ueber die Philosophie der Religion*, vol. 2 (Hamburg: Meiner, 1966), 74 ff., 98 ff.

Notes

**13** See Rudolf Otto, *The Idea of the Holy* (Oxford University Press, 1950), 77 ff.

**14** See e.g. S. R. Hopper on Jeremiah 31:15-22: 'Though our home is nigh, we are somehow far from it . . . Our faces are not radiant with the glow of the Lord's goodness. Between us is a desert of exile. Within us is the abyss of emptiness.' (*The Interpreter's Bible*, vol.5 (New York: Abingdon Press, 1956), 1031 ff.)

**15** John Bright, *Jeremiah* (New York: Doubleday, 1965), 287. See also the amazingly similar comments in the *Cambridge Bible Commentary*. E. W. Nicholson gives only the factual material about the Rachel passage but writes of Jeremiah 31:31 ff. as follows: 'This short passage is one of the most important in the Book of Jeremiah. Indeed, it represents one of the deepest insights in the entire prophetic literature in the Old Testament.' (Jeremiah 26-52.) (Cambridge University Press, 1975, 70.)

**16** Arthur Weiser, *Das Buch des Propheten Jeremiah* (Goettingen: Vandenhoeck & Ruprecht, 1952), 293 ff.

**17** Yechezkel Kaufmann, *The Religion of Israel* (University of Chicago Press, 1960), 75.

**18** Weiser's commentary on Jeremiah 31:31 ff. concludes as follows: 'According to Luke 22:20 and I Cor. 11:25 Jesus, in instituting holy communion, understands Jeremiah's promise of the new covenant as fulfilled in his own person . . . '.

**19** *Truth and Method* (New York: Seabury Press, 1975), 244. On the hermeneutical issues emerging here and elsewhere in this book, see also *To Mend*, part IV, chapter 11.

**20** Quoted by Irving Greenberg, 'Cloud of smoke, Pillar of fire: Judaism, Christianity, and Modernity after the Holocaust', *Auschwitz: Beginning of a New Era?*, E. Fleischner, ed. (New York: Ktav, 1977), 9 ff.

**21** G. Tillion, *Ravensbrueck* (New York: Anchor, 1975), 77.

**22** See further below on the two meanings of this appellation.

**23** Johann Baptist Metz, 'Oekumene Nach Auschwitz: Zum Verhaeltnis Von Christen und Juden in Deutschland', *Gott nach Auschwitz: Dimensionen des Massenmords am Juedischen Volk*, no editor listed (Freiburg: Herder, 1979), 124. Metz's essay also condemns any Auschwitz 'theodicy' as 'blasphemous', rejects all 'triumphalist [Christian] metaphysics of salvation', and insists that henceforth Christians must listen to Jews in their search for truth. This the Carmelite nuns failed to do before their decision to establish a monastery at Auschwitz.

**24** The cited Luther passage, taken from his *On the Jews and their Lies*, is quoted by H. Bornkamm, *Luther and the Old Testament* (Philadelphia: Fortress Press, 1980), 189. On the same page he also cites Luther's much-cited remark: 'I am hostile to Esther and II Maccabees, for they judaize too much and display much pagan conduct.' (II Maccabees is, of course, not part of the Jewish canon.) In view of Luther's own siding with Haman, perhaps most striking is the following: 'It [i.e., Esther] judaizes immeasurably. They [i.e., the Jews] love this book very much. Like

*117*

# Notes

Haman (Esther 6:1 ff.), they really wanted to be exalted.' (Ibid.) Elias Bickermann writes: 'If we accept the postulate that the New Testament is hidden in the Old Testament and the Old Testament is revealed in the New Testament (Augustine), this view of Luther's is both logical and legitimate' (*Four Strange Books of The Bible* [New York: Schocken, 1984], 212). For a Barthian attempt to 'baptise' Esther, see Wilhelm Vischer, 'Esther', *Theologische Existenz Heute*, No.48, Munich, 1937. Arbitrary – nay, untenable – Vischer's effort nevertheless deserves respect for its political courage as well its theological ingenuity: note the year and place of its publication.

A balanced but, after the Holocaust, insufficiently searching essay is Bernard W. Anderson, 'The place of the Book of Esther in the Christian Bible', *Journal of Religion* 30 (1950), 32-43.

25 Thus Elie Wiesel sums up an incident reported by Rabbi Shim'on Huberband, a chronicler in the Warsaw Ghetto until he was murdered. See his *Kiddush Hashem* (New York: Ktav, 1987) and the *New York Times*, 17 January 1988.

For all of his siding with Haman, Luther and the 1937 *Martin Luther Universitaet* must be sharply distinguished. In his preface to *Martin Luther: Theologie des Kreuzes* (Leipzig: Kroener, 1933) editor Georg Helbig cites Luther as follows: 'The Germans will not give up their sins until an external enemy will vanquish their rage. The just punishment that is prepared for the world if it forgets and despises the Word of God – this will come upon Germany after my death.' Helbig wrote his preface on 'Luther's birthday' in 1932. (10 November: Any connection with 10 November 1938, the day after *Kristallnacht*?) Surely the book was published after 30 January 1933. What Helbig meant by citing this text – on his first page! – is beyond a shadow of doubt. What happened to him?

26 Richard Bauckham's yet unpublished 'The Book of Esther and the Jewish Holocaust' ends as follows:

> In the light of this history [i.e., of persecution culminating in the Holocaust], Christians would do well to read Esther precisely as a Jewish book whose presence in the Christian Bible claims Christian attention. They should read Esther as the book which Jewish inmates of the Nazi death-camps were forbidden to read, but wrote out from memory and read in secret on Purim.

Bauckham's is a ground-breaking essay. His astonishment at how little post-war Christian attention Esther has received is reminiscent of Eberhard Bethge's view that Dietrich Bonhoeffer, were he alive, would be amazed at how 'seamlessly' Christian theologians carried on their business after 1945 where they had left off in 1933.

I am encouraged by how close Professor Bauckham's views are to mine, and am grateful for our all-too-brief conversations during my Manchester visit.

Somewhat encouraging is also the following in B.S.Childs: 'The inclusion of Esther within the Christian canon serves as a check against all attempts to spiritualize the concept of Israel – usually by misinterpreting Paul – and thus removing the ultimate scandal of biblical particularity.' (Op. cit., 606.) I say 'somewhat encouraging' because – as the parenthesis indicates – for all his monumental attempt to do justice to the Jewish Ta'nach as well as the Christian Old Testament, Childs either backs away from the Holocaust or ignores it.

27 Peter Sichrovsky, *Schuldig Geboren* (Koeln: Kiepenheuer & Witsch, 1987).

28 Dr Mengele smiled when in 1944 three-year-old Susan and Hanna were brought to him: his experiments with twins! Sometimes during the nine months that followed – this surviving Susan hated to admit at the 1989 Jerusalem conference on 'Mengele's Twins' – the doctor acted as though he liked them. This did not stop his 'experiments' – invariably without anaesthetics. During these months the two were kept in a cage. The *Jerusalem Post* account of Susan's testimony (8 September 1989) ends as follows: 'Mengele wanted to know how young humans react to severe confinement.'

29 Bab.Talmud, Sanhedrin 96b, also Gittin 57b.

30 *Job* (Edinburgh: T. & T.Clark, 1904), 346. That scholarly expertise does not guarantee profundity when required is illustrated by M. H. Pope on *Job* 42:13. On what seems dubious philological evidence he translates 'He had twice (?) seven sons and three daughters' and comments: 'In any case, the number of daughters remains the same. A larger number of girls would have been a burden rather than a boon . . . The pagan Arabs used to bury unwanted daughters at birth for fear that the family would be impoverished by feeding them or later disgraced by their conduct.' (*Job* (New York: Doubleday, 1965) 289, 291.) Disappointingly, Rashi *ad locum*, too, has the sons doubled; but at least he spares us the 'pagan Arabs'. See also *To Mend*, 132 ff.

31 Theodor Adorno, *Negative Dialektik* (Frankfurt: Suhrkamp, 1975), 355. The translation is mine.

32 On this subject see further my *WiJ*, ch. 13.

33 *At the Turning* (New York: Farrar, Straus & Young, 1952), 61.

34 On the subject of the last several paragraphs, see further *WiJ*, Part III.

35 *The Gates of the Forest* (New York: Holt, Rinehart & Winston, 1966), 255.

36 Bab.Talmud, Pessachim 117a.

# INDEX OF NAMES

# DATE DUE

| NOV 1 2 2000 | | | |
|---|---|---|---|
| DEC 2 3 2003 | | | |
| MAR 1 4 2005 | | | |
| MAR 1 4 2006 | | | |
| | | | |
| | | | |
| | | | |
| | | | |
| | | | |
| | | | |
| | | | |
| | | | |
| | | | |